BETTY GOLD
1324 PACIFIC AVE.
VENICE, CA 90291

# The Dance, Art and Ritual
## of Africa

# Michel Huet

# The Dance, Art and Ritual of Africa

Introduction by Jean Laude     Text by Jean-Louis Paudrat

Translated from the French

**Pantheon Books**
**New York**

All rights reserved under International and Pan-American Copyright
Conventions. Published in the United States by Pantheon Books, a
division of Random House, Inc., New York, and simultaneously in Canada
by Random House of Canada Limited, Toronto.
Originally published in France as **Danses d'Afrique** by Société Nouvelle
des Éditions du Chêne, Paris.

Grateful acknowledgment is made to the following for permission to
reprint the material listed below:
    Dominique Darbois, for photograph number 35
    Georges Duchemin, for photographs numbers 17 and 18
    Bernard Curé, for the photograph on page 19

**Library of Congress Cataloging in Publication Data**
Huet, Michel, 1917.

    The Dance, Art and Ritual of Africa.

    Translation of **Danses d'Afrique**
    1. Dancing-Africa. I. Paudrat, Jean-Louis. II. Laude, Jean. III. Title.
GV1705.H8313   703.3'196   78-7248

ISBN : 0-394-50272-8

Manufactured in Switzerland

FIRST AMERICAN EDITION

# Contents

# Preface by Michel Huet

The liberation of my country in 1945 struck a deep echo in my heart, as it did with so many of my generation who were young at that time. Our freedom had been restored to us at last; we were free to live anew, and to dream of great undertakings and great discoveries.

As a young professional photographer with a thirst for adventure, it seemed to me that the whole world had become my oyster. I have always felt this urge to discover new lands, ancient civilizations, traditions and ways of life different from our own; beauty in all its forms. I felt, strongly if not very clearly, that our Western industrial society was going to have a marked effect on countries which up till that time had been remote from our form of progress. The values of such societies were in danger of changing or even disappearing altogether, and it was up to us to capture them by photography and perhaps, by this means, save them.

Then came the question: on which region should I set my heart? South America, Asia, Africa . . . all of them appealed to me equally.

It was a photography assignment in the African Art Museum that quite by chance decided me. When I was first interviewed by the Museum Curator in his office, I was fascinated by the feel of Africa that came to me in that room. It opened up new horizons. Later, in the Museum itself, the masks and statuettes seemed to me to spring to life in the brilliance of the spotlights. They seemed to be bearers of a message. I was overwhelmed by the extraordinary beauty and harmony of their forms. I could sense in them the deeply reverent attitude that the sculptor had had towards his work. Names hitherto unknown to me began to dance before my eyes. Fang, Baoulé, Senoufa, Bambara . . . who were these mysterious people who had produced things that aroused such feelings in me? It was as if a dialogue had begun to take place between the masks and myself, and there was no way for me to find the answer except to go to Africa. In other words, I had fallen well and truly under the spell of that country.

Ethnology was out of the question for me. Detailed comparative studies of ethnic groups were best left to the scientists. I myself, at any rate to my own way of thinking, was no specialist but an all-rounder. So from Senegal to the Congo Basin, from the sand dunes of the Sahel to the Gulf of Benin, through the sultry forests and across the thorny bush, free from prejudice of any kind, I came to know the land of Africa. I had only one aim: to get the feel of the continent and to translate this feel into images.

I was beset by difficulties. The first was that in order to be independent I had to be able to get around the country. Nowadays there are splendid chromium-plated caravans, beautifully equipped with every conceivable gadget, available for people to drive to camp sites along newly asphalted roads. In the 'fifties things were very different. There was an ill-defined, 'corrugated iron' track; a bridge that had collapsed; a fallen tree—victim of a recent storm—blocking the way; numerous breakdowns; sandstorms. These were everyday occurrences.

But I had to have some vehicle of transport, and I chose a Renault Savanah. It had a super 85 engine, although I couldn't say much for the Gregoire suspension, which broke down with monotonous regularity and gave me a great deal of trouble. Inside the car I carried a camp bed and a mosquito net, a case of cooking materials and tinned food, a water filter, and a substantial supply of petrol. If I didn't, like the snail, actually carry my house on my back, at any rate I carried it behind me. I was

7

thus equipped to stop wherever I chose and to wait as long as was necessary for favourable climatic or psychological conditions. I taught myself to be patient, and I had the means whereby to exercise that patience.

As regards photographic equipment, I started off with two excellent Rollei 6×6, one for black and white pictures, the other for colour. I have never had any reason to regret choosing this relatively large size, which was so appropriate for the records that I was to make. Later, however, I was tempted by the Hasselblad because of its ample lens possibilities and its interchangeable magazines. It offered a wide range for the choice of viewing angles and in the quality of film used. The wide angle gave a depth of field and a rapidity in approximate focusing that allowed me to concentrate all my attention on filming. The coloured films, once exposed, were kept among my clothes for safety and sent by air to France at the earliest possible opportunity.

I soon became aware that the music and the dances were much more than mere entertainment, that they were an expression of the very essence of African life. Marriages, funerals, harvest festivals, initiation ceremonies—all were carried out to the rhythm of the drum, the blowing of the horn, the tinkling of iron bells, and accompanied by a display of masks, in accordance with a ritual that has remained unchanged throughout the ages. I also realized that I must not interrupt at the wrong times and that I must not disturb the people in the course of their agricultural labours. In short, I had to do my best to be present at the right moment, which was generally during the dry season. That was the time when the village was most accessible. Once the crops are safely stored away to meet the daily food requirements of the village, then the people are free to turn their thought and energies to the initiation ceremonies, free to carry out the homage due to the souls of their ancestors, free to pay the funeral tributes due to one or other deceased chief.

At such favourable times I would hang around hopefully, and it very often happened that I was able, without any prior arrangement, to enter spontaneously into the dance activities. But I could not just drop in by chance every time. Had I relied on this, it would have taken me a lifetime to collect all the documents I wanted, so fate had to be given a helping hand now and again.

The Civil Services gave me very valuable help. At that time most of the commanding officers had heard of or even attended one or other of the ceremonies. They would accompany me to the village chiefs and smooth the way for me. After that came the discussions. Of course I had the advantage that these 'men of the dance' were always delighted to get into action, and so I received a much warmer welcome than would have been extended to a tax collector! But since African dance has a religious content, it is not performed for just anybody, and I

had first to win the confidence of the people and establish a friendly relationship. A village would immediately offer me the use of the visitor's hut, and they could see from the equipment I carried that I was perfectly prepared to wait for as long as was necessary. I was a reliable but exacting visitor, letting the villagers understand that I was not going to be satisfied with just a few pirouettes but that I wanted the full ceremonial with the relevant masks and costumes.

In some cases it was essential that a consecration ceremony should take place for the rites. Among the Baoule, for example, the procudeure was to pour a calabash of palm wine over the tomb of Queen Pokou and ask whether her spirits would give their assent. They gave their assent . . .

There were also cases in which we, the outsiders, were included within the African taboos. If, for instance, there were certain masks that women were forbidden to look upon, then I certainly would not expect my wife to be an exception to this rule. She often had to stay in the background, but sometimes, and particularly in North Cameroon, she got her own back. Here there was a certain village that had up till that moment been completely isolated from Western civilization, and so far as the villagers could remember, nobody there had ever set eyes on a white woman. The revelation was sheer delirium. The women squatted round her in a circle, clucking and chuckling their rapture and praise between their labrets. Everywhere she went she was greeted with spontaneous demonstrations of welcome. Some of the children even called her by her Christian name and to many of them she became known as 'Maman Ghislaine'.

But to revert to the subject of capturing the images of the dance, the preparations for this and the unexpected setbacks. In Benin, at the very heart of the Yoruba country from which we had such high hopes, all the village dancing had been suspended for several months. The village had not paid its taxes and seemed unlikely ever to be able to do so. Long and exhausting discussions took place, and hints were dropped, in the best diplomatic tradition, that allowed the village chief to hope that the dance might be worthy of a gift, and that this gift could take the form of a fiscal remission. All turned out well. We had our dance, the Yoruba received their gift, and the Civil Service received its taxes.

Then there was sometimes a problem with the costumes. Certain dances had fallen into disuse and the costumes had been abandoned. Never mind, we said; we had plenty of time to wait for any renovations to be made. So the village, bubbling over with enthusiasm, would get down to cutting out hides and decorating them with cowrie shells, monkey hair or vegetable fibre, in order to revive the neglected rites. In the Upper Volta it was most impressive to see the long line of villagers strolling into the bush at dawn, going off to pick the tender green Karité leaves that were used for the costume of every dancer. Tradition decreed that every dancer had to be covered from head to foot with these leaves, so the size of the crop can be imagined!

On other occasions our plans were upset by taboos of a different kind. In Chad, under the influence of a Protestant mission, the wonderful Korbo women of the Dangaleata ethnic group covered their traditional costumes with plain boubous. These traditional costumes were reminiscent of Egyptian bas-reliefs, and the basketwork head-dresses and the heavy anklets were only to be seen as part of the whole costume. With the help of my wife I managed to persuade these women— about thirty in all—to take off their boubous and uncover their gorgeous traditional dress.

Those who are to take part in the dance arrive one by one. In the Northern Cameroons, the long line of the Fali stretches out along the mountainside, converging on the tree of the dance. Neighbouring villages empty themselves of their population. The very forest seems to approve when the sacred grove opens to let out its mystery. The mask emerges, surrounded by its musicians. The nobles take their places in the assembly, the children fidget about, the tom-tom gives out its first hesitant throbs . . .

Slowly the dance becomes organized. Every dancer moves to his appointed place, and it is very rare, in these group ceremonies, that any one individual member is allowed to be the star of the show. Only the masks—and who knows who they cover?—take up a leading position, but like everybody else they have to submit to the dance and the rhythm that is progressively imposed by the music.

Those were rare and precious moments, never to be forgotten. I pushed myself to the limit, rushing from one side to the other, clambering up on whatever came to hand in order to take overall views of the dancers, even sneaking right into their midst to catch a particularly striking movement. I surpassed them all in my enthusiasm. At first they were amused by it, and then it seemed to be catching, because they were fired by it too. The same force seemed to be driving us all, and suddenly the dancers would no longer look on me as a 'foreigner', an outsider, but accept me completely, even forget I was there, as the basic meaning of the dance became more and more clear.

But such times were not always conducive to professional photography. The light was not always ideal. What I wanted to do was to single out certain elements, to emphasize certain gestures. So when the rhythm slowed down and I felt some lessening of the intensity of the action, I took things in hand. Gently but firmly I disposed the essential elements under the required light. I arranged them and asked them to begin again. I became, in fact, the moving spirit of the occasion, arranging

it for the requirements of the photography.

Meanwhile my wife was trying to collect information, which was no easy task. African society is composed of various ethnic groups, and a European mind has difficulty in making its way through this labyrinth. And even when friendly contact is made, there is no way in which the uttering of a few sentences can convey the deep reality of Africa, the roots of which reach back into forgotten ages. The Africans are kind people, and this kindness inclines them to agree with everything you say. It might be due to such simplicity, or it might perhaps be due to subtlety, that they always answered in the affirmative, agreeing both with a statement and with its opposite.

The proceedings came to an end with the ritual dispensing of gifts, which consisted of new banknotes. These were either handed to the village chief, who then shared them out, or, in accordance with a customary practice, they were discreetly stuck into the women's head-dresses.

Then we would part on excellent terms, promising to return. I have in fact kept that promise, since my travels have often led me back to the same ethnic groups, always with renewed interest and always making new discoveries.

What advice can I offer to the many people who would like to discover Black Africa as I did, who would like to see at least a part of what I was lucky enough to see? Nowadays everybody is talking about such matters as cotton crops and coffee-processing, of vegetable oils and of foreign markets, of towns expanding into great cities. Such things form the present-day reality, it is true; but this reality must not be allowed to conceal the deep and fundamental reality of Africa, this fundamental Africa which has recently been in eclipse, but which nevertheless retains the firm conviction that she must keep alive her own origins and remain true to them.

Africa does not show herself readily. Sensation-seeking tourists will only get from her what they look for: sun, coconut trees, rest, 'exhibition' dances. It will be for the more discriminating traveller to discover the old forgotten ways, to adapt himself to the rhythm of the country, to get to know the Africans, their dignity, their philosophy. But to be such a traveller there is one thing that is essential: you must travel with an open mind and, above all, an open heart.

Michel Huet

# Introduction by Jean Laude

No subject can be properly studied and appreciated without some knowledge of its history. The dances of sub-Saharan Africa are no exception to this rule, but it is only recently that they have entered the realm of specialized studies. The reason for this is partly technical. New techniques have been developed for recording both visual and sound images in a manner that is essential for a study of dance. These records have made possible the work of detailed analysis and comparison which could not have been undertaken without such materials.

But these technical improvements, while very necessary, do not by themselves account for the undertaking of a serious study of African dances. Pictures and sound records require interpretation, and this interpretation requires a knowledge of the historical background. In the present state of research into this topic our knowledge is still fragmentary, but what we know leads us to believe that these dances have a much greater significance than appears on the surface; that they are, in fact, repositories of meaning.

It was at the end of the Renaissance and the beginning of the Baroque period that objects originating in sub-Saharan Africa were first imported into Europe. Most of these were made of ivory by craftsmen in the kingdom of San Salvador and the coast of Guinea. The musical instruments were of particular interest. They were mainly horns carved out of elephant tusks, and the pictorial symbols were concerned entirely with the art of hunting, evidence that the horns symbolized the privileges of a particular social class. Reproductions of these instruments are, however, included in treatises dealing with the making of music, notably those written by Michael Praetorius (1619) and by Sandrart (1679). Other careful and detailed reproductions of the different instruments are to be found in the chronicles of travellers, sometimes printed, sometimes handwritten[1]. These coloured drawings or engravings show musicians playing solo or with an orchestra. Finally, the records kept by explorers invariably included descriptions of dances and ceremonies that the authors happened to have witnessed.

As these illustrations and descriptions became more widely known, the reaction of the Western world towards them became more and more rejecting and repressive. In the United States of America, laws were passed forbidding the slaves who had been brought there from Africa to dance in groups. The attitudes and fantasies of Western peoples about the human body clearly emerge from the wording of these nineteenth-century laws. There is a striking and fundamental ambivalence in the Westerner's viewpoint: fear on the one hand, fascination on the other. The choreographic performances described in the records would, it was feared, result in a lowering of moral standards and in uncontrolled or 'animal' sexual behaviour.[2]

During the Renaissance and Baroque periods interest in African culture was primarily centred on the musical instruments and the dancing. The reasons for this do not concern us here, but this type of interest became less predominant until, during the first decades of the twentieth century, it was the sculptured object that was most highly favoured. For the Western world, 'African art' came to mean the masks and the statuettes that were so easily exported. These coincided with the Western concept of a 'work of art'; a finished product, an actual tangible and visible object that could be contemplated and admired. This rather narrow and limited notion of 'art' has become outmoded in the light of later ethnological and other studies. Both in Europe and in the United States, the notion of what constitutes 'art' has been expanded to include other spheres of human activity, including the movements of the body.

In the case of African art, then, it was clear that this could not be restricted to the sort of sculptured objects found in museums or in private collections. And under this wider definition of art it also became clear that the masks, for example, could not be fully understood and appreciated when isolated from the costumes of which they formed a part. In fact they needed to be considered in the context of the whole complex and spectacular ensemble for which they were made. No problem, whether scientific or non-scientific, can be dealt with quite apart from its context. The recent interest among Western peoples in the dances of sub-Saharan Africa is itself part of a larger question—the question of the whole attitude of Western civilization towards the human body. And it also shows the willingness of the Westerner to regard such body movements as a form of artistic expression.

This collection of photographs by Michel Huet is extremely valuable for a variety of reasons. Their quality is immediately obvious and needs no stressing. The photographs speak for themselves, but there are one or two comments that perhaps need making. Some of the photographs have captured moments in rituals or ceremonies which are, in fact, in some cases no longer carried out. The printed document has outlived tradition and human memory, but it is no substitute for them. The other point is that Michel Huet has taken care not to confine his illustrations to the most spectacular and tense moments in a dance, but has made a series of pictures of the same rite so as to give us a synthesis of the different phases of the dance.

This having been established, it is possible to proceed to an analytical and comparative study and draw up a repertoire of steps and figures.

The quality of these photographs must be instantly apparent to everybody. The interest that they awaken can be scarcely less widespread. There is nevertheless some risk that they could be seriously misunderstood by those who are unfamiliar with sub-Saharan African culture and that they could even reinforce some existing prejudices. The Colonial texts present these dances as spontaneous and purely instinctive manifestations of these *bamboula*. It cannot be emphasized enough that this is completely untrue. The dances and ceremonies, certain moments in which are reproduced here, are by no means the simple expression of collective energy as was once so thoughtlessly believed. On the contrary, they are strictly regulated according to criteria which, while differing from those which govern Western choreography, are no less precise and imperative. In addition, these dances are institutionalized. They are only performed on certain occasions and at certain times, and they involve clearly defined objectives. Jean-Louis Paudrat has attempted to link up each series of pictures with the significance attached to them by the ethnic group in question. These texts accompanying the photographs are clearly and concisely written. The information they convey has been derived from both the most ancient and the most recent ethnographic sources. They are not mere accessories to the photographs, but are essential explanations of the ritual situations depicted in the illustrations. And this is not merely a collection of exotic photographs. Texts and illustrations taken together can lead to a fuller understanding of the people in question.

## Archaeological and Iconographic Evidence

Sculpture is by no means characteristic of all parts of sub-Saharan Africa, but dance and its accompanying symbolic representations is universal in this part of the world, so much so that it may well be regarded, in all its varieties, as the distinctive and typical feature of African culture. There is evidence, proto-historic if not prehistoric, that dance existed in the eastern Sahara when that region was able to sustain life. In the Tassili, numerous wall-paintings have been uncovered, representing ceremonial scenes in which masked and unmasked dances play an important role. Among these is a large frieze found at the outpost of Sefar. On this frieze are three masks closely resembling those still used by the Chokwe people of Angola. At Aouanrhet a tall masked figure, overprinted by a round-headed woman, was found. Other paintings are less clearly defined and it is not possible to ascertain whether they represent masked dancers or mythological beings.[3] But there has not been any systematic scientific research carried out on these sites, particularly as regards the bones, tools and food remains found there, and one cannot therefore go further than make a very general statement: at a time before the Roman occupation there were people living in this part of the Sahara, people whose rites seem to be comparable with those now practised in sub-Saharan Africa.

Moving to other regions, Jean Paul and Annie Lebeuf have unearthed in the Chad, from sepulchral mounds built by the ancient Sao, clay statuettes which are believed to be representations of masked dancers and which can be traced back to the twelfth and sixteenth centuries.[4] In many of the regions of sub-Saharan Africa there are sculptured statuettes representing instrumentalists. In Benin, for example, there are bronze statuettes of horn-players, and also a *bas relief* plaque like the one in the British Museum which shows a tambourine player in the midst of a group of percussion instruments. Not to mention the famous kuba effigy (Zaire) of King Kata Mbula, renowned for his prowess on the drums. And two examples can be given from the Dogon, of a harp-lute player and two seated xylophone players, both in the New York Museum of Primitive Art.

The musical instruments themselves are works of art, whether drums with the entire surface covered with mythological representations (Baule), or shaped like an antelope (Zambezi, Museum of Man), or ivory horns (ancient kingdom of San Salvador), or carefully carved, engraved, or decorated (Benin), or harps with necks decorated with a human face (Mangbetu) or whose blades are fixed to the bust of a female statuette (Zande, Royal Museum of Central Africa, Tervuren).

It should be remembered that in the African cosmogony, the instruments and the music played on them have an important and sometimes decisive role. Thus, in the case of the Dogon, three successive 'messages' or 'ways of speech' are revealed. The first is in the form of a seed, the next in the form of a loom, and the last an armpit drum. It is surely not without significance that these three 'messages' have been delivered in an order which itself holds great meaning. This sequential order in fact evokes a genetic conception of the human world. It rests with the armpit drum, with the volume of sound, to found and create, in the myth, a three-dimensional space. But it also gives body to the latent vibrating energy. In the seed this was in a state of dormancy; in the loom only two-dimensional—the zig-zag pattern formed by the movement of the thread along the warp.

All such relevant facts should be collected and analysed before being considered as a whole, but even as they stand, they already give us some clue into the more significant characteristics of African life. The very fact that in Black Africa there is no culture that does not, or did not, practise dancing and that in most of these cases the dance is a necessary accompaniment to the music, is evidence of the important part played by these choreographic performances in sub-Saharan Africa. Furthermore, in the myths and in the African cosmogony, musical instruments are believed to be highly specialized agents determining the genesis of the nature-culture dichotomy. We may therefore ask quite specific questions about the functions of musical instruments in these societies. These functions include both those consciously and institutionally assigned to the musical instruments, and also those unconscious assumptions and associations that underlie African creativity.

*Masques Dogon* by Marcel Griaule is probably the only work to contain a systematic study of dance and choreography in sub-Saharan Africa with regard to both the individual steps performed by each type of dancer and to the movements of the group.[5] The author suggests that the word *awa*, meaning in the Dogon language 'the mask society', could be the equivalent of the Greek *cosmos*. This is an all-embracing term, and not only the particular rite or 'show', but also the whole institution, must be looked on as a whole. We come here into realms of meaning that it is very difficult for Western minds to grasp. We are dealing with phenomena which cannot be conceptualized in Western terms without depriving them of that which gives them their unique quality. When we study African dance we have to forget completely the sort of dichotomy that is familiar to Western thought: the opposites of secular and religious, profane and sacred. Such opposites can only exist in a dualist structure. In our present state of knowledge, we have no reason to suppose that there is any such element in the sub-Saharan cultures.

The ensemble, as revealed in the word *awa*, manifests itself first and foremost in the 'show' itself, which includes masks, dance, music, and the recitation of myths. It consists of a complicated network of elements, each of which reinforces its profound unity. Every element, from costumes to choreographic figures, from polyrhythm to choral or solo singing, has its place in an overall meaningful system, a strict code linking the world of daily routine activities to the cosmic order originally conceived and drawn up by the creator or the god. The unified code also links the events that occurred at the time of creation with their repetition, in symbolic form, in the world of today. Every tiny detail is heavy with specific meanings, which transform themselves according to the different combinations of which they form part. It may well be that what still puzzles us about the painted representations of ceremonial celebrations and the sculpture of Sao masked dancers or instrumentalists could be explained by this principle of repetition. There is a gap which is only too apparent between our knowledge of the functions of the objects sculptured in sub-Saharan Africa and the meanings that seem to be assigned to them.

These objects, or representations, are not anecdotal: they do not tell a story in the sense that we understand it. Nor are they purely aesthetic, aiming to present an image to the eye. It is not a question of the painter or the sculptor making a representation of an act that has been or will be staged, thus emphasizing its essentially transient aspect. On the contrary. These representations ensure the permanence of the act. In other words, they are an assertion of the central role assigned to dance ceremonies in daily life and of the continuity of traditional cultures. They embody a conception of time which is unfamiliar to us, and to which I will return later.

## Masks

Whereas dance is present in the ritual ceremonies of all the sub-Saharan cultures, the wearing of masks is far from being universal in this region. Their use therefore stands out as a distinctive element which should be examined. Equally noteworthy is the fact that there is very great variety in the numbers and types of masks to be found in those societies that do use masks in the ceremonies. The Dogon of the Bandiagara Cliff region use a great corpus of masks, classified according to the role played in sacred operas. In other areas there is less diversity and they are fewer in number. The neighbouring Kurumba, for example, have only the beautiful antelope shape on top of the cap placed on the dancer's head.

How can we account for such diversity? Can we, for instance, attribute the rich variety of Dogon masks to the fact that they have been settled in that region since the twelfth century of our Western era, and have had all this time in which to conserve, develop and enlarge their own particular type of culture? In fact it does not appear to be a case of preserving their culture in all its original purity. Quite a number of its elements have actually been taken over from neighbouring cultures such as the Kurumba, the Mossi, the Peul. So the rich iconography, the variety of styles, and the complexity of the underlying myths seem to be a result of the fact that the Dogon, far from remaining isolated and self-contained, came into close contact with other peoples, and either borrowed certain cultural features or else were obliged to submit to them.

As late as 1931, Marcel Griaule had noticed a 'Madam' mask, caricaturing the European women who occasionally accompanied the Colonial officers on their tours of inspection. This was not just a matter of reacting to one particular incident, but the mask forms part of the category of Dogon masks that depict the 'foreigner', whether it be Peul, Saman or European. In fact, all aspects of life, as revealed to the Dogon in their legends, have their own significance, their own place in the unity that is the whole. Thus all external elements, whether imposed upon the Dogon or voluntarily taken over, are absorbed and integrated into their myths and iconography, nourished, diversified, and made into a part of the whole. These external elements are not looked on as something alien and exotic, but as something to be adapted and reinterpreted to suit the Dogon system. Examples of such external elements taken over in this way are certain masks of the Gelede community in Yoruba territory. These masks are surmounted with symbols of European objects: sewing-machines, motor-bikes, sunglasses and tropical helmets, and sometimes even aeroplanes.

One point needs stressing here. The arts of sub-Saharan Africa have far too often been regarded as being rigidly traditional and conservative. They are indeed traditional, but only in a special sense. Indeed, if we consider the few examples available from a particular population, we find that this material is not as uniform as was supposed, but contains marked variations. Everything points to the fact that innovations have been brought into the myth and resulted in a change in the iconography. Such changes are always concerned with the overall structure of the institutions and the myths, which is gradually transformed by the alien elements that it has absorbed. This evidence that traditions can thus be modified obliges us to reconsider the whole question of functionalism in African art. We must not look on its traditions and manifestations purely from a synchronous point of view, treating them as rigidly fixed at a certain period of time, as ethnology tends to do; but we must look on them as phenomena that can change over a period of time. In other words, we must look at them with the eye of a historian. History deals with phenomena as they occur and as they change, and endeavours to trace and understand such changes, whether social or cultural.

Let me illustrate this process by quoting the example of the Bobo from Upper Volta. These people are basically farmers and are of paleonigritic origin. In their earliest times they wore leaf masks. Such masks are still used in the purifying ceremonies held from time to time in recognition of the wrong done to Nature by man's seasonal labour and the sins committed by man. It was not until much later in their history that they took over from the Dogon the huge blade-shaped wooden masks associated with the ceremonies devoted to ancestors and to the dead. Very likely this change took place when the country was invaded by the Manding. There would be no formal take-over by a centralized government or authority in a society that had no formal political institutions, not even of the loosest federal kind. Each village was completely autonomous, and it would be into such a social structure that the new elements were absorbed.[6]

Our study of the masks associated with the Dogon myth gives us access to one of the oldest layers of sub-Saharan culture: that concerned with those who practised agriculture. Among the paleo-African populations, the invention of masks seems to be linked first and foremost with purification rituals. There was no ambivalent attitude towards Nature. Nature was felt to be essentially good. The practice of farming was an offence to Nature, and this offence had to be paid for. But whatever measures were adopted to make atonement, they could not be expected to save man from Nature's punishment. So the institution of the Mask society, which aims to purify the earth and those who have defiled it, coincides with the appearance of Death. This close relationship between the purification rites and the funeral rites poses a problem. From our own observations of the working of the human conscience, we may conclude that once men believe that they have committed a serious outrage, they will search everywhere for means of atoning for it and lessening their own guilt. In the example under discussion, death would be regarded not only as a punishment for this outrage, but also as a means of conceiving procedures that might mitigate its effects. So instead of the classical opposites of 'nature' and 'culture' we have them merged together into a structure in which the two terms do not exclude each other but, on the contrary, give rise to productive tensions.

Thus the leaf mask of the Bobo attracts the particles of evil spirits which roam the villages, and the fibre skirts of the Dogon are covered with symbols of guilt derived from the primordial wrong perpetrated by the incestuous jackal. Around this original myth structure new elements cluster, and gradually they combine to form the complex and impressive structure that Marcel Griaule studied and that he called the *awa*. After these preliminary remarks we should be in a better position to look at the problem of cultural identities on the one hand and that of functionalism on the other. A few comments on the morphology and the typology not only of the masks, but also of the systems of which they form a part, will also be of use at this point.

Let us try to make a rough classification of the masks, always bearing in mind that the objects in question cannot be dissociated from the costume of which they form an integral part. These masks would appear to be the product of the peculiarly African imagination, and the most surprising formal inventions are linked to a diverse iconography. The masks may be grouped into six main categories: (1) masks made from leaves, wicker-work, or cloth; (2) facial masks; (3) helmet masks; (4) helmet peaks; (5) blade-shaped masks; (6) masks surmounted by sculptures.

The symbols used are as varied as the types of masks. There are animal masks of all kinds, masks in the form of a man, masks representing fantastic and heterogeneous beings, masks crowned by group sculptures or by objects such as houses, seats, sewing-machines, motor-bikes, and so on.[7] There is, however, no one mask-producing population in which the entire range is to be found. For instance, there is no trace of any helmet mask in the Dogon territory, while these are frequently used, even as a matter of privilege, among the Yoruba, the Fang and the Ba-Teke. Some categories appear to be limited to certain cultures. Thus the blade-shaped masks belong to the relatively homogeneous ethnic groups of the Dogon, the Bobo and the Mossi.

The same remarks apply to the iconography of the masks. Among the Dogon and the Yoruba, for example, a wide range of objects and symbols are represented. Other populations such as the Kurumba have only one or two models. The variety of forms seems to follow from the diversity of themes. If there is only one iconographic model in any given culture, then there seem to be few variations in style between one object and another. Such small variations as there are, are probably due to the hand of the individual sculptor. But where the masks deal with a lot of different themes, then there is also to be found a wide variety of objects within each theme.

This is a matter on which systematic research would be well worth while. If a sufficient number of objects were available to be classified into different themes, and the varieties of style within the theme then studied, it should be possible to try to trace the evolution of these masks within the different cultures of which they form a part. A contribution would thus be made towards the study of iconography in the Panofskien sense, and this sort of double classification should make possible a deeper study of cultural identities.

The foregoing remarks should have made it very plain that we cannot regard cultural identities, doctrines, myths, customs and rites, as being permanently fixed in an unchanging tradition. On the contrary, these phenomena should be examined in the light of a culture's potentiality to absorb elements from the world itself, and thus nourish and enrich itself. It cannot be stressed too much that those engaged on research in this field should not confine themselves to the kind of ethnographic studies that regard these traditions as fixed and unchanging. It is absolutely essential to carry out these studies concurrently

with historical research, so that problems can be viewed in perspective and new questions be posed.

Admittedly this will lead to great difficulties of methodology. Both written and pictorial records are extremely rare and sporadic. They are derived mainly from past research, and one cannot expect any great degree of reliability from records of traditions handed down by word of mouth. These two big disadvantages are partially counterbalanced by the fact that there is an abundance of specialized monographs that gives us the chance to draw up a corpus of knowledge and to cross-check, thus establishing a firmer basis for critical analysis and the processing of information. There is still a great deal to be gathered from this new science of African archaeology.

Ethnographic studies and historical research have been much too circumspect and half-hearted in the field of the art of black Africa. This is partly because both ethnologists and historians have been suspicious of the kind of interest that African art has aroused in Europe, an interest that has so often not been scholarly or serious at all, but merely a matter of a current trend or fashion. It may well be that the so-called critical studies of African art, written by people who were ill-informed and who took care never to place the objects in their true environment, drove the historians and the ethnologists to consider the dance and the sculpture from a purely religious and social viewpoint and to make no attempt to trace their significance for history as a whole. In so limiting themselves, however, they neglected to take into account the fact that art, in whatever form—choreographic, sculptured, architectural—serves as a record, as archives, for those who produce it. This is indeed one of the functions of the art in question, just as its objective is to perpetuate, by repetition, historical and mythological events. Finally, we have good reason to believe that the changes in the actual forms of the objects are symptomatic of changes in the actual social systems.


## Dance and the 'Person'

Whether performed with or without masks, the dance ceremonies take place at fixed dates marked in the ritual calendar. Sometimes there is a long lapse of time between them—perhaps even as much as several decades; at other times, as in the case of a death, the date is not predictable. The liturgy stresses closely hidden themes of a religious nature. The dance ceremonies have definite functions in the life of the group, and their nature and complexity depends on the events that have given rise to them.

The dance is an integral part, but not the whole of the ceremony. This 'whole' includes costumes, music—either orchestral or choral—figures and story-telling, either singly or all together. The ceremonies are conducted according to a scenario which differs from one population to another and within the same population, depending on the events to be celebrated. The ceremonies do not occur in spaces that have been exclusively set aside for this purpose, but in the area where daily life takes place: in the village itself, in its main square, or in its immediate surroundings of country, sacred wood, or forest. Occuring as they do at specified dates, these ceremonies are felt to be significant landmarks in the sequence of days, contrasting with the monotonous routine of daily occupations. One may say that they give a structure to time, but not in the automatic manner that a clock does. They do indeed give shape to time, but they also have a deep internal meaning that forms one of the fundamental features of mythic philosophy.

As the date of the ceremony draws near, food and drink are accumulated in the village over and above the quantities that would normally be consumed. The 'festival' is thus felt to be an occasion for excess, for consuming and exhausting the accumulated resources. This feature is linked on a structural level with another feature, one that is characteristic of sacrifices, and that apparently derives from other concepts. The purpose of a sacrifice is to release the 'immaterial' from the animal or, to put it another way, it is to bring under control an energy which if allowed to remain at liberty might bring evil on the community. During the relevant rites, this energy is controlled and mastered by whoever is doing the sacrificing. Thus one of the functions of the masks and the costumes of which they form a part is to stabilize and completely absorb this energy, thus protecting those who might be invested with it and distributing it for the benefit of the whole community. These purposes are served by the ritual ceremonies.

The energy, however, even when fixed does not cease to be dangerous. The costumes of the dancers are evidence of this danger. Those wearing the most dangerous masks protect their bodies with long garments that hide every inch of skin. In the Dogon region, the wearer of the great sirige mask has to perform certain exercises during which his throat is uncovered, and for these an assistant stands in front of him to conceal this vulnerable spot. Still in Dogon territory, should a woman inadvertently see a mask forbidden to her as to any uninitiated, she becomes 'possessed' and is integrated as a yasagine (sister to the mask) into the *awa*.

The energy which is released at the death of every living creature, whether animal or human, must be trapped and controlled, and then exploited by redistributing it for the benefit of the entire group. It may well be that this energy stands for Nature, which can be both life-giving and benevolent, malevolent and dangerous, at the same time. The concept is personified. In fact, the notion of 'person' seems to be fundamental to African wisdom, an essential part of its organic and genetic conception of the universe. Not only all living things, but also what Western minds regard as abstract categories, such as time and space, suffer a loss of their vital forces and must be periodically regenerated. Hence the notion of rhythm, which finds expression in sculpture as well as in those manifestations where the body and the music work together.

We must bear in mind the foregoing in order to understand the complex pattern of the dance of possession, where energy is the focal point. While performing these dances, the participant and also the assistants may, under certain circumstances, become the 'horse' of a spirit. This is clear from the word Yoruba used in the Orisha cult, in the Haitien Voodoo cult, or the Bresilian candomble. After the dancer has gone through a fit of hysterics that deprives him of consciousness, he then opens himself to the spirit by performing regular repetitive movements which enable him to be conducted by the spirit and to imitate its physical singularities.[8]

Here is surely ample material for research. Sometimes parts of the dance ceremonies are transformed into images. This has happened in the case of the Dogon statuary and in all probability in the case of the Tellem, their ancestors. Some of the statuettes represent the descent of the spirit Nommo, with raised arms, into the hogon's skull. There is at least one example, in the Museum of Primitive Art in New York, where this religious and temporal chief is represented with his skull sectioned. In its symbolic form the excision of the encephalon, which is the seat of all mental powers, indicates the ataraxia aimed at during the last stage of initiation among the Bamana, and which is represented by the ox. This state cannot be reached until the ultimate stage of initiation. It is not given, it does not come naturally, but only at the end of a long process covering an entire lifetime.

While the possession dances are being performed, the 'horse of the genie' has possession of the code of gestures, attitudes and conduct of the genie, and his acting will ensure that the incarnated spirit is recognized. But the dancer does not know, before he launches himself on to the dance area, whether he will be possessed or by whom. He must therefore have at his command the complete range of steps and figures of whatever personality it is who will ride him. This knowledge is not innate, but has been communicated to him beforehand through the appropriate musical rhythms. There is no spontaneity about it. On the contrary, the performance depends upon a detailed and profound knowledge of what being is likely to be the possessor, of what may cause the body to be the temporary incarnation or abode of another being. It should be noted that although the possession is effective, genuine and violent and is certainly not feigned, and that it shows the clinical symptoms of epilepsy, it nevertheless has distinctively theatrical features about it. To be more precise, the knowledge of the conduct peculiar to each genie has been acquired and the conduct of the genie is 'staged' in a definite context.

Michel Leiris, in his study of the zar possession cult in Ethiopia, has pointed out the ambiguous character of this phenomenon which takes place in a region where what seems to be a completely subjective means of expression is, in fact, part of a system of symbolic representations, elaborated and acknowledged by the group. These possession dances, and also the initiation dances and the funeral dances, whether performed with or without masks, represent a two-way process of transformation. They transcend the ordinary social life, with its industry and its peaceful organization, by their excesses and their expenditure of material and spiritual energy which announces the sudden and spectacular intrusion of nature into culture. But at the same time they demonstrate the power of culture, or order, to control and reorganize the chaotic powers. This control is established in two ways. Either through a systematic whole in which each gesture, each attitude, each movement holds a meaning that is understood by the whole group in varying degrees, in accordance with the stage of initiation reached by the person concerned; or else in the form of a rigid set of rules which puts strict limits on the time allowed for the festival period.

It will be evident, therefore, that one cannot apply the nature-culture antithesis to these ceremonies, with the one excluding the other. Rather is it a case of these two aspects working together. The excesses and the exuberance of Nature, with their risk of exhaustion and carrying within them the seeds of their own destruction, are brought under control and regularized to a certain degree. On the other hand the social rules and regulations of Culture, which might be felt as oppressive and arbitrary if never lifted, are temporarily put aside, and this very putting aside reveals afresh how very necessary for daily life these rules are. The lifting of various taboos, particularly sexual taboos, during festival periods is particularly significant. It is not simply a question of opening up a safety valve and liberating the natural impulses when the pressures of conforming to social standards become too heavy. There is more to it than that. It is a matter of reinvestment in the social system, of re-

commitment to it; of legitimizing it, as every human creation needs to be legitimized from time to time. If it were not for this element of reinvestment, it would simply be a matter of giving way to chaos and disorder. But the opposite is true. The function is to reduce the devastating effects of such excesses and disorder.

For the Bamana, man is the seed of the universe. This is a very significant and expressive metaphor. It unites mankind with other species, with the whole corpus of living beings, and the inference is that the whole evolution of mankind, both material and spiritual, is a slow germination process whose pattern is familiar to agricultural communities. Man does not exist as an individual, but as a person. Marcel Mauss called attention some years ago to the fact that the etymology of the word 'person' is in fact mask. The Latin per-sona indicates the artificial face worn by actors, through which the sound of the voice is emitted and amplified.[9] And according to Marcel Griaule, the dancer plays the part reserved to the wooden object, the sculptured mask that covers his face or head.[10]

Now I must return to that genetic conception that dominates the thought of the sub-Saharan farming communities: the universe in which man is but a seed follows, in the course of its evolution, a process identical to that which causes plants to germinate, grow, wither and die. This process is periodically repeated, as at each new season the plant emerges again and starts a new cycle. The structure appear to be similar to that found in the classical myths of death and rebirth or, on the cosmic level, to the idea of eternal return. The similarity is only apparent, for it is not possible for every new birth to be repeated on the same identical plane as the previous one: it takes place at a slightly superior degree.

## Knowledge and the Body

To assert that man is the seed of the universe is to assert the responsibility he has to assume in the creative processes Nature, left to itself, tends by its own abundance and its own excesses to consume and destroy itself. Man's responsibility is thus defined. In conjunction with the universe, through a network of analogies that attach him to it, he becomes both a part of it and a reduction of it. He is responsible for ensuring that Nature is not offended nor rendered barren; he must make amends if offence is given, must heal the sterility. And he must also try to prevent any regressive or degnerative process. His role is to compensate for the depreciation of the universe, of the cosmic order; he is not merely to maintain it as he found it, but to enrich it and take charge of its evolution, with rites performed at the beginning or end of initiation rituals, during the time of sowing, or at the end of the harvesting time. These rites may be concerned with initiation or with atonement and they may, like those of the Sigi in the Dogon region, take place only every sixty years; they may occur on the occasion of the enthronement of a king or a chief; they may be connected with a military campaign or as the necessary accompaniment of funerals. But whatever be the function or the occasion, these dances, masked or unmasked, recreate in the social context a partial or complete representation of the original myth.

The re-creation does not involve an identical repetition. Granted that microcosm and macrocosm, earthly order and cosmic order, are in close symbiosis, then an event occurring in one of these orders has an immediate effect on the other. Thus the reproducing on earth of events that occurred at the origin of time, means that they are brought forth again regenerated, since they correspond to a pre-established order determined by a god or a creator. This regeneration involves a periodic recharging with Nature's flood of burning energy, an energy that needs ordering and channelling because, in the legendary ages when man came forth, it took offence at this birth, and nothing but purification and atonement rites can make amends. Looked at in this perspective, the dance ceremonies have a dual role: that of mastering the 'natural' impulses on the one hand, and that of knowledge on the other.

A Gnostic hymn of the eleventh century attributes the following sentence to Christ: 'He who does not dance ignores all that goes on around him.' It is the dance that sets off the process of elucidating, perpetuating and transferring knowledge—the original knowledge that German philosophy calls *Urnatur*. The dance gives the community a framework of common experience. It legitimizes, through living reference to the original events, the social and religious codes that must be respected and observed. But the knowledge thus diffused does not form an inert body of strict and unvarying dogmas. In fact the dances themselves take place on a border line that paradoxically both severs nature and culture and unites them, which indicates the serious risks that the actors incur and from which the dances are supposed to protect them. The role of the initiation is to transmit and legitimize the rules with which the candidates must comply. This will certainly not be accomplished in one stage. In fact, taking into account the economic investment required in dues of all kinds, initiation can extend over a whole lifetime. The myths become richer through criticisms and interpretations. They expand to take in new elements; they encompass a reality whose complexity is forever increasing.

Both the dancer and the audience may be in positions of danger. Hence care is taken to exclude the uninitiated from certain ceremonies. The participants may be trapped by Nature. If a possession crisis occurs by accident, then it must be immediately integrated within the system and become part of the institution. Or it could be that a rite miscarries, which means that it has failed to capture the necessary forces to revitalize the laws of the community, and the community will thus be deprived of the hoped-for benefits.

The evolution of knowledge, whether individual or commonal, is a slow process, as slow as the growth of the plant from the seed, as slow as the successive stages of initiation. No one can reach the superior stage without making his way up from the bottom. There is no hurry and there is no point of breaking off. There is only an awareness, at every living stage of the road followed, of adhering to the reality of the world as it is. It is a regular progression into which all events are to be slowly integrated, and all temptations to play or to go astray must be ignored.

The very first stage of initiation seeks to inculcate such an attitude. The Bamana, for example, give their adolescents a collection of tools, grouped in chronological order and showing in a concrete manner the slow evolution of techniques. But this progress does not appear to follow a linear reasoning. It follows a rhythm analogous to the spiral germination of plants which, in the Dogon philosophy, is contained both in their myths and in the plastic structure of their statuary.[11]

In various aspects of social life, and particularly in the masked or unmasked dances, mental structures in general seem to be adjusted to a twofold conception of rhythm, based on the nature-culture duality. This rhythm is often extremely vigorous and demands a great expenditure of physical energy on the part of the musicians and an extremely high volume of sound. This is produced by the human voice, solo or in chorus, by orchestras consisting mainly of percussion instruments, by wind instruments and, less frequently, by stringed instruments.

Sub-Saharan music is made up of complicated polyphonic chords based on accent sequences. The music of the pygmy tribes of the Gabon forest is essentially voal, and here Herbert Pepper[12] was able to record songs with a construction similar to that of overlapping eight-voice fugues. The resonant flow of sound, in close accord with the devouring energy which sweeps through Nature, is built up in rhythmic elements. The repetition of these rhythmic elements conveys the continuity of these violent forces; at the same time, it conveys the network of meanings connected with the linking of the microcosm to the macrocosm, the earthly order with the cosmic order.

18

A specific rhythm is assigned to every mask and to every step that the dancer performs; this rhythm characterizes the 'spirit' and indicates its presence. In the possession dances, when the genie has made himself known, the orchestra plays the music which is appropriate to him and which identifies him. As I have stated earlier, should the ceremony result in the breaking through of another genie, this other is incorporated into the ceremony and institutionalized. These ceremonies have none of the spontaneous and anarchic character so thoughtlessly attributed to them by the Western world. The slow process of initiation, with the strong rhythm marking important moments, tempers and moderates the natural impulses in the spiral manner referred to earlier. It channels them into tensions, subordinating their intensity into the required efficiency. There is thus a regulating and organizing factor in the force of the rhythm, in the surge of the dance, either group or individual, and in the music as a whole. This has as its aim the giving back of the natural energy to the community which, in turn, will distribute it among its members at these periodic ceremonies. The regulating and organizing factor is based on the classification system acknowledged by the group, the system which governs the relationships between men, and between men and other living things, as well as the cosmo-biological correspondences.

The body is thus trained to be part of a complex network of analogies established with the universe, but the thinking behind it is not dualist. Physiological tendencies and social rules are both taken into account in this education of the body. It is acquired by means of an apprenticeship during which the steps and figures are taught in relation to the complete ceremony, and it is the duty of the initiation schools to explain their meaning. In this education of the body the opposing concepts of chaos and order, disorder and regulation, are brought together in a way that incites the body to work through its own tensions.

The ceremonies based on this education of the body are not 'shows' in the sense that a Westerner would use the word. They are performed in the course of the everyday life which they regenerate and re-style. They force the audience to revert to its own culture, to recognize its collective identity. In Europe and in the United States there is a tradition of choreography and of the 'show' which is entirely different from that of sub-Saharan Africa. In the Western world the body is seen through a dualist mental structure as opposed to, or subordinated to, the mind. Contemporary artistic movements in the Western world show a rather naive yearning for those ritual celebrations in which art is indistinguishable from life, a yearning for some sort of deep communion between man and the universe. It must be said to the credit of those carrying out research today in the sphere of choreography and the theatre, that they are genuinely trying to link our own way of thought with the other way, and are not simply fascinated by the exotic for its own sake. But this research is being carried out at a time when both the Western world and sub-Saharan Africa are in a state of crisis, and when Africa, although trying to remain true to her cultural identity, is progressively giving up her practices, or at any rate transforming them.

I will conclude with the sentence with which I began this essay: that no subject can be properly studied and appreciated without some knowledge of its history.

J. Laude,
Professor of Art History,
Paris University I
Panthéon—Sorbonne

## Notes

1. Cf. on this matter, the invaluable research work of Ezio Bassani: *Scultura africana nei musei africani*, Bologna, Calderini, 1977.

2. In his remarkably well-documented thesis entitled *Le Dénigrement* which was defended at Paris I University, Panthéon, Sorbonne in June 1974, J. L. Paudrat has analysed these logistics with great accuracy and has devoted a chapter to this subject, 'La forêt danse'.

3. Lajoux, D: *Merveilles du Tassili*, Paris, Ed. du Chêne, 19   . pl

4. Lebeuf, J. P. and A. M.: *Les arts des Sao*, Paris, Ed. du Chêne, 1977. pl. 65, 66, 67

5. Griaule, M.: *Masques Dogon*, Paris, Institut d'ethnologie, 1938

6. Le Moal, G.: 'Rites de purification et d'expiation', in *Système de signes*, Paris, Hermann, 1978

See also Paudrat's essay: 'La sculpture africaine: tradition et création', in the Barbier-Muller Collection *Sculpture d'Afrique*, Geneva, 1977

7. For details of these types of masks, see J. Laude: *Les Arts de l'Afrique Noire*, Paris, Livre de Poche-Art, 1966

8. For a description and analysis of these phenomena, see Griaule, M.: *Arts de l'Afrique noire*, Paris, Ed. du Chêne, 1948, pp. 100-103; Leiris, M.: *La possession et ses aspects théâtraux, chez les Ethiopiens de Gondar*, Paris, Plon, 1958. Cf. also the films of Jean Rouche, *Yennedi*, which deals with the possession dances of the Sorhai from Niger, and *La betaille du grand fleuve* and *Les Maîtres Fous*.

9. Mauss, M.: 'Une catégorie de l'esprit humain. La notion de personne, celle de ''moi''.' *Journal of the Royal Anthropological Institute*, vol. XVIII, London, 1938

10. Griaule, M.: *Arts de l'Afrique noire*, p. 103

11. See Laude, J.: *African Art of the Dogon. The myths of the Cliff Dwellers*, New York, Viking Press, 1973

12. Pepper, H.: 'Anthologie de la vie africaine (Congo, Gabon).' Moyen Ducretet-Thompson, 320 C 126-127-128, Artistique (with booklet)

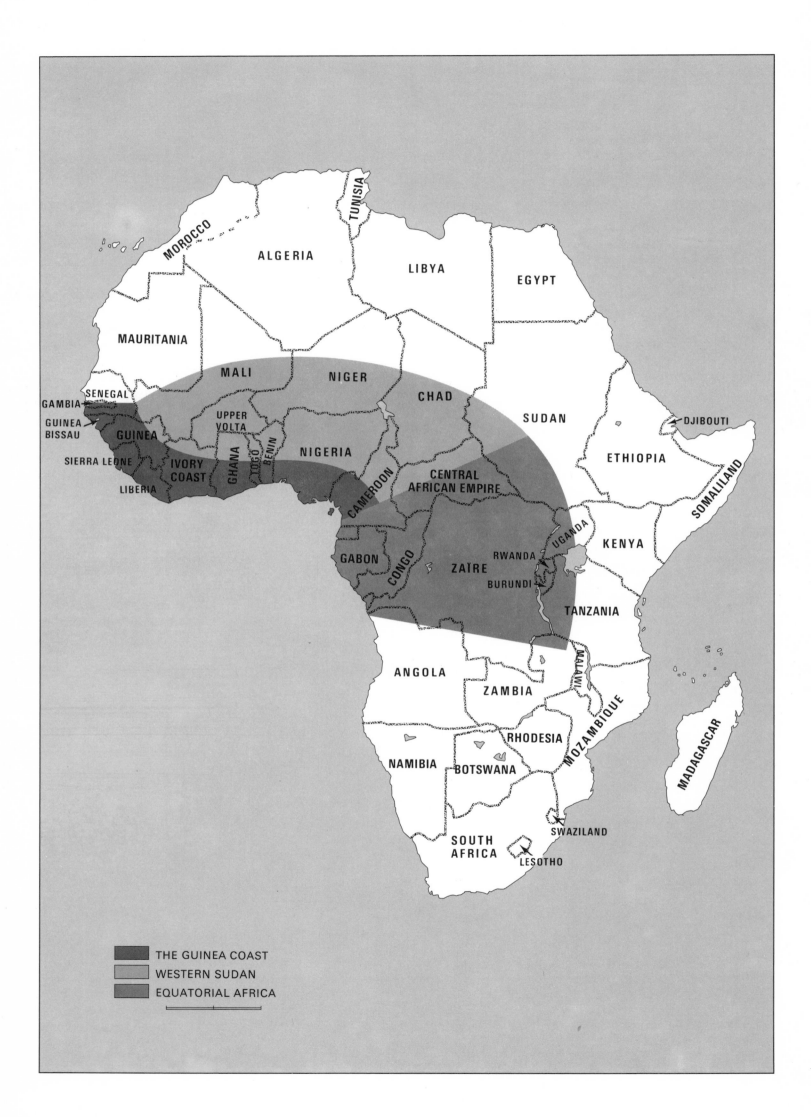

MOROCCO
TUNISIA
ALGERIA
LIBYA
EGYPT
MAURITANIA
MALI
NIGER
CHAD
SUDAN
SENEGAL
GAMBIA
GUINEA
BISSAU
GUINEA
UPPER
VOLTA
SIERRA LEONE
IVORY
COAST
GHANA
TOGO
BENIN
NIGERIA
LIBERIA
CAMEROON
CENTRAL
AFRICAN EMPIRE
DJIBOUTI
ETHIOPIA
SOMALILAND
GABON
CONGO
ZAIRE
RWANDA
BURUNDI
UGANDA
KENYA
TANZANIA
ANGOLA
ZAMBIA
MALAWI
MOZAMBIQUE
NAMIBIA
BOTSWANA
RHODESIA
MADAGASCAR
SOUTH
AFRICA
SWAZILAND
LESOTHO

THE GUINEA COAST
WESTERN SUDAN
EQUATORIAL AFRICA

# THE GUINEA COAST

1: DIOLA
2: KONIAGI AND BASSARI
3: FULANI
4: KISSI
5: BAGA AND NALU
6: TOMA
7: KONO, DAN AND GUÉRÉ
8: GURO
9: BAOULÉ
10: ÉWÉ
11: FON AND YORUBA
12: BAMILÉKÉ AND BAMUN

0      500      1000 km

# The Guinea Coast

## The Coast of West Guinea

### Senegal

*Diola* (Lower Casamance)

1 The kabisa is a great wooden drum. Placed under a canopy, beaten by hand or with sticks, it announces the important moments in the social life of the Diola community.

With a monotonous beat in six-eight rhythm, on the note of G sharp, it tells of the death of a village notable. It is sounded at the start of a funeral ceremony or during the final rites of mourning. But it is also often beaten to celebrate a particularly profitable hunting expedition.

To make and use the kabisa is the privilege of the initiated, and it has a religious function, as evidenced by its use during funeral ceremonies and during the rites celebrated to atone to the bush spirits.

But the drum is also used during the season of wrestling matches. This is a time of rejoicing in the village following the gathering of the harvest, and it opens to the sound of this drum.

3 The wrestlers, or atuma, are boys of between sixteen and twenty. They are arranged into pairs of contestants, each wrestler representing a village or a district. The contest itself is soon over: each match lasts only two or three minutes. It has to comply to a strict set of rules. From early childhood, the Diola are taught to practise the twenty essential holds that they have to know in order to take part in the katag.

The strength and agility of the atuma are well revealed in these contests, with their quick seizing of the initiative and their speedy parrying of holds. They are not, however, regarded by the Diola as expressive of long-lasting rivalries between districts or villages. On the contrary, they appear to act as necessary preambles to friendly meetings between the young people of the different communities. In some respects they reinforce the solidarity of these groups.

In the dance that follows the katag, therefore, the victor and the vanquished will be seen to come together in brotherly friendship.

2 As soon as the wrestling matches are over, three drums are placed in the centre of the public square where the matches have taken place. One of these, a split drum called the koukou, smaller than the kabisa, gives its name to the dance.

4 In the wrestlers' dance, the dancers alternately advance and retreat. During the pause between these two movements the drums cease, and the jingle of the bells and rattles that the atuma wear round their waists or ankles can be heard.

The costumes and ornaments of the atuma are peculiar to the katag-koukou performance. The shaven heads of the dancers are topped by a tuft of hair, a few red and white feathers, and occasionally a ring of cowries. Around the neck, arms and legs there are a variety of necklaces and bracelets made of metal, beads or palmyra fibre. To the wrestler's belt, the ékei, are fixed a string of bells, a sort of tail woven in red yarn, and the sheath of the weapon which will be brandished only during the dance.

The resonators of the ankle rattles are made of braided palmyra fibre, although nowadays this basketwork is often replaced by empty condensed milk or beer cans.

*Bibliography*

L.V. Thomas, *Les Diola*. Mémoires de l'IFAN, 1959, Paris-Dakar

### Guinea

*Koniagi and Bassari* (Youkounkoun Region)

The Koniagi and the Bassari live in the north-western foothills of the Fouta-Djalon. Closer and more numerous contacts with the outside world have brought about a more rapid change in the traditions of the Koniagi, the men of the plains at the foot of the Temgué mountain range, than in those of the Bassari, the men of the bush.

The clothes worn by the Bassari are not ostentatious. The men wear a penial support made of plaited palmyra leaves and a triangular piece of antelope hide covers the buttocks. The Koniagi, in contrast, often use woven cotton and imported materials.

The head-dress is very nearly identical in both societies. Both sides of the head are shaven, and the remaining hair on top is either braided and arranged into a long central crest or else into a thin braid wound round the skull and ending in a small tail a few inches long that lies on the nape of the neck. Bands of blue or yellow beads, or even silver or copper coins, adorn the hair. During the initiation ceremonies of the Koniagi, the young men 10 wear the daka, a huge ceremonial crest draped with red and 11 white material edged with feathers. 12

The daka is an exaggerated form of the crest hair-style, and it signifies power and beauty. Beads are much used in the Koniagi costumes, while the Bassari society makes greater use of bracelets, necklaces, belts and circular leg ornaments made of 17 copper or aluminium. 18

The Koniagi, under the influence of the Malinké, have adopted musical instruments such as the xylophone or the lute-harp, the use of which is widespread throughout West Africa. But the Bassari, apart from the great hide drum which is beaten with the 13 flat of the hand, limit their use of instruments to those specific to 14 their culture. An example of these are the long ridged bamboo 16 scrapers or bamboo tubes, which are neither musical bows nor

15 bark cithers, and on which one of the bamboo fibres has been separated and stretched at each extremity with thin wooden supports. The musician, whose mouth acts as a sound box, strikes the blade with a hard wooden stick.

*Bibliography*

M. de Lestrange, *Les Coniagui et Bassari*, PUF, Paris, 1955

## Peul (Labé Region)

Among the Fulani of the Fouta-Djalon region, the dyeli, who are the musician caste, use the monochord vielle and the soron, a nineteen-chord lute-harp, together with big semi-spherical
6 drums, beaten alternately with tongues fixed at the ends of fibre braids.
5 In the course of the performance the dancer unfolds his wide
7 pleated trousers, which are gathered at the ankles. He uses a
8 whistle and a half-calabash, beating with his rings on the
9 external side of it.

## Kissi (Guékédou Region)

When they return to the village from the forest where they have undergone the first stage of initiation, the young Kissi boys per-
19 form a dance. Their heads are shaven, some of them wearing a woman's false hairpiece, and their bodies are covered with a net
20 and a long skirt of raffia fibre. They advance in single file to form a
21 circle. Then they go forwards, turn, and jump on the spot, following the increasingly rapid rhythm of the split drum, the gbassia. This labia drum is hung horizontally under a canopy. The 'orders' that it gives out are punctuated by two small cylindrical hide drums.

*Bibliography*

A. Schaeffner, *Les Kissi, une société noire et ses instruments de musique*, Hermann, Paris, 1951

## Baga and Nalu (Boké and Boffa Region)

24 The mask that is named yoké, klokui or kumoé, according to its extension, should not be confused with the well-known nimba mask. Both are busts of a female figure, but the smaller sized yoké is worn by a single dancer. The head, which is small and set on top of a long ringed neck, and the breasts, which are heavier and bigger, place it in a different ritual context from that of the nimba. The nimba is associated with the rice production and consumption cycle, and pertains to notions of fertility and abundance. Its meaning is deeply linked to the Mother-Earth conception. But the yoké, which is danced by the Komo Faré to a brisk rhythm during the celebration that marks the end of the female initiation rites, evokes the young girl rather than the mature mother. Its main function is to encourage motherhood and protect from sterility.

The koni, or tyamba, and the dudu masks are now reserved 25 exclusively for entertainment purposes. They are common to the 26 Baga, to the Nalu and to the Islamized Soussou. The miming of 27 the dance illustrates the legend of the encounter of Koni, the hornbill bird, 'spirit of good', with Dudu, the 'wicked man of the forest'.

Banda masks have often been associated with monstrous 28 figures, probably because of the intricate overlapping of dis- 29 similar pieces, the abundance of decorative detail, and their 30 imposing size. They combine anthropomorphic elements such as human eyes, nose and head-dress, with zoological elements such as crocodile jaws, antelope horns, chameleon and snake symbols, but they must not be regarded as the result of a meaningless fantasy.

The banda should be looked on as a plastic reconstruction of the fundamental principles which rule the world of the Nalu. These masks illustrate the way in which the three worlds of man, the village and water complement each other. Hence the crocodile and the snake; the bush; the chameleon and the antelope. In former times, nobody was allowed to see the banda except those initiated into the secret society of the simo. More recently these masks have, so to speak, been deconsecrated. They appear in dances performed before a wider audience, always on important occasions in the life of the Nalu, such as funerals, the harvest, circumcision, and protective rites against the dangers of the bush. The carvings are heavy and the wearers of the masks must execute a rigidly exact set of figures. The banda mask dance, or banda faré, is therefore only performed by specialists, two or three young men from each village. The banda must be shown from various angles: horizontally, that is to say, in profile; then vertically, which is full face, and finally, involving a complete rotation of the dancer, all sides at once.

*Bibliography*

G. van Geertruyen, *La Fonction de la sculpture dans une société africaine*, Baga-Nalu-Landuman, *Africana Gandensia No. 1*, Gand, 1976
B. Holas, 'Danses masquées de la Basse-Cote', *Etudes guinéennes No. 1*, Conakry, 1947

*Toma* (Macenta Region)

The Toma live on the Liberian border in the south-east of Guinea, in the heart of a high forest surrounded by mountains. Despite their apparent isolation, their culture is not confined to their own tribe, but is shared with other ethnic groups, both neighbouring and more distant. Examples are the stilt mask or laniboi, which is also to be found among the Kono and the Dan, and the okobuzogui, the secret mask, similar to the banda mask of the Nalu.

35 The ouenilegagui, however, seems to belong exclusively to the Toma. This costume refers to the bird of the original myth, a bird that brought power to human society.

The body is whitened with kaolin and covered by a feathered coat. The head is crowned by a kind of clay helmet with a tuft of feathers, and the ankles are circled with iron bells. Thus equipped, and carrying a staff in one hand, the Bird Men emerge from the forest. There are two occasions on which they appear. The first is after the death of a zogui, that is, somebody initiated into the secrets of the forest spirits. On the second occasion they accompany the young candidates for initiation, the bilakoro, to whom they will act as monitors during the physical trials.

During their initiation the bilakoro will learn among other things the language of the labia drum.

It is this instrument, a hollow wooden cylinder split along nearly its whole length and beaten by two hard wooden sticks, that governs the dance of the Bird Men. The two lips of the drum are of varying thickness, and by combining the different sounds obtained the musician 'talks' to the dancers and transmits the figures to be performed.

*Bibliography*

P.D. Gaisseau, *Forêt sacrée*, Albin-Michel, Paris, 1953

*Discography*

*Musique Toma*, Musée de l'Homme LD4, side II, No. 9

## Guinea and the Ivory Coast

*Kono-Dan-Guéré* (Triple Border Region)

1. *Guinea Kono* (Village of Nzo)

In the village of Nzo a festival takes place during the period following the rice harvest. It is an occasion which reunites the kono masks, dancers and musicians from the Vepo district.

The most important moments in the festival are marked by the display of the nyon hiné, the nyon néa and nyon kpman masks; the performance of the nyon kwouka or masks with stilts, and the dances of the women's association, Tokpa.

The male mask, nyon hiné, with its cylindrical head-dress adorned with cowries and its black face half human, half animal, is accompanied by an interpreter and an orchestra of ivory horns, 55 the furu, and two bara drums. His partner, nyon néa, the woman mask, participates in the dance. She wears a conical-shaped hat 34 on top of a beautiful oval face. The clean outlines of the bright patina of the female face are in striking contrast to that of the male, where the beak or mouth in the lower half is wrapped in an imposing beard made of colubus hair.

It is the function of this amazing couple, who appear in broad 31 daylight before the entire assembled community, to bring back to the kono initiates the fundamental experience of their second birth within the Poro. Admittedly, the néa is no longer the 'Mother of all Men', who gave birth to the 'New Men', marking them with her claws, nor is the hiné the relentless master of the initiation rites. Nevertheless, these two masks, though deconsecrated and exposed to the gaze of all comers, still evoke the beginning and the end of a cycle. The presence of néa and hiné during this period of prosperity bears witness to the fact that the society has been able to discover the necessary means of diminishing the evil effects of uncontrolled Nature. Thus the face and ornaments of néa, suggestive of the force of human institutions and in particular the Poro, at the same time are expressive of beauty and serenity.

Nyon kpman, before the colonization of Upper Guinea, was a 32 particularly awe-inspiring war mask. In order to secure its assistance, the military chief used to spit the purple-red juice of 33 slowly-chewed cola into its face.

When the function of the nyon kpman was reduced to that of a mediator, the ritual spitting was replaced by the pinning of a red cloth to its wooden face. This red cloth, cut from the Senegalese infantry's red chechias, was used up till the 'fifties, so that nyon kpman continued until that time to be reminiscent of its ancient usage as a war mask.

The well-known mask with stilts of the triple border territory 47 originates in kono country. That interest in this mask has never to 55 flagged is borne out by the fact that its use spread to the Toma in the west and to the Ivorian and Liberian Dans in the east. But the importance of this mask does not lie simply in the naive delight aroused by its acrobatic stunts. Its designation, kwuya-gblen-gbé, evokes a reference to its height, and also places it in the category of symbolic representations, nyomou-glé-gué.

In certain traditions it is said to be present during the boys' initiation ceremony. It is also said that the making and preparing of this mask for an outing can only take place on the outskirts of the village. Finally, any display of the mask must first be approved by the local religious authorities.

In spite of the fact that the mask is used over a wide area, the basic elements in the costume are very similar. These include a conical-shaped hat with cowries, grains, leather and cloth rags, surmounted by a tuft of white ram's hair. The dancer's face is hidden under a net of palm-tree fibre, while long braids hang at mouth level on either side of the face. The upper half of the costume is made of a blue-and-white-striped cloth shirt with the cuffs sewn together, and bells and a raffia skirt are attached to the belt.

The stilts, which are sometimes as much as two metres high, are cut from the banana tree because of the strength, flexibility and lightness of this plant. They are usually covered by long trousers. The feet of the dancers rest on two lateral supports, and the uprights are tied to the shins to give greater freedom to the knees. The sounds uttered by the 'long mask' are high-pitched and grating, and it is sometimes accompanied by a chorus of young men. The musicians beat small drums and shake rattles.

To execute the figures of this dance is a constant challenge to the laws of balance. Rapid steps, crossing of legs, leaps and pirouettes are carried out to the point of overbalancing.

Over and above these feats of acrobatic skill, the kwuya dance is a symbolic representation of the wisdom of the group. It is the means by which the kono society proves to itself that it can escape from the gravitational forces of the earth. This search for equilibrium outside normal conditions, this breaking through the barriers, show that man has the power to thwart the traps that are constantly being set for him by the 'witches'.

**56**
**57** Dan society also includes the Tokpa women's association,
**58** which is nowadays called the 'Knife Society'. It is an assembly of mothers who are at the same time initiators of young girls, midwives, and responsible for the excision act.

One of its functions is to act as village purifier. For example, the zolé, who rules over the association, has the task of pouring on to the ground the liquid which has power to force away evil spirits coming from the bush.

In the dance that follows the end of the girls' initiation rites, or at childbirth, the symbol of fertility is shown to the sounds of rattles, bamboo-wood drums, percussion bovine horns, double
**58** bells with external clappers, and ankle bells. This symbol is cone-shaped, made of blackened soapstone, and is inlaid with cowries. It evokes the secret instrument, the gonda, through which the voice of the Mother, nyon néa, is heard during the poro.

## 2. *Ivory Coast, Dan and Guéré* (Duékoué-Bangolo Region)

**36**
**to 46** The spectacular demonstrations of the 'Serpent Society' are common to the Dan, Wobé and Guéré territories. Today, the reputation of these groups of 'jugglers of girls' extends well beyond the west of the Ivory Coast.

In past times the preparation of the pharmacopoeia for the curing of snake bites was the privilege of a specialized group of healers. Immunized against the effects of the poison, these healers would publicly exhibit venomous snakes. They were called the simbo, the snake-charmers, and during their impressive dances they were accompanied by very young girls who also played with these dangerous creatures.

This, then, is the original reason for the behaviour of the jugglers' societies. Simbo is the name for the men aged between twenty and thirty who perform with the young girls, the sang- **42** noulou. In one of these acrobatic dances the simbo's young **43** partner twines herself around the dancer's body. In another **45** dance, performed by one of the young girls on her own, her **36** sinuous and undulating movements evoke those of the serpent. **to 41**

The importance of these dances goes beyond the fascination cast over the audience by their acrobatic or juggling feats. The Serpent Society expresses the values universally accepted by the group: self-control, body control, will-power, courage.

These values are never so much in evidence as when two **44** simbo, facing each other at a distance of a few metres and **46** holding a sword at arm's length, casually toss to each other the young, impassive, sangnoulou girl.

## 3. *Ivory Coast, Guéré* (Guiglo Region)

From Liberia in the south-east, where they are called Kran, to the Ivory Coast in the north-east, where the northernmost group is called Wobé, the Guéré inhabit a forest region, access to which remains difficult even today.

These people possess several cultural traits in common with their western neighbours, the Dan, although there is a difference in dialect, with the Guéré belonging to the krou group and the Dan to the mandé-fu group. Apart from this, the Guéré use, in current religious and social life, masks that are uniquely their own: the song mask, blé gla, and the wisdom mask, gbona gla, are examples of these.

Blé gla, the 'singer', frequently identified with téhé gla, the **60** 'dancer', is a red, white and black mask. The sculpted part is adorned with a cowrie tiara and a beard of brass bells.

To the accompaniment of three men shaking rattles and a singer replying in a nasal voice, blé gla sings and dances for the pleasure of the villagers when an event of importance—a death, for instance—creates social tensions.

Such tensions may persist and intensify for a variety of reasons: an unsatisfactory settlement of a conflict within the group, for example: or disease or death, the causes of which may be blamed on witchcraft; or a bad harvest. In such cases gbona gla, the great mask of wisdom, is called forth. Its impressive face, **61** with two pairs of tubular eyes and gaping mouth, is topped by an imposing head-dress made either of touraco or fishing eagle feathers.

Gbona, leaning on the staff of power and authority and surrounded by his guardians and interpreters, progresses at a dignified pace. The myth of the origin of the masks explains the respect and awe they inspire. At the beginning of the world, man, blended with the animal kingdom, was subject to incessant conflicts that defeated his efforts to establish a stable, coherent human society. The creative god, Nyon sua, in his mercy despatched some good spirits to the earth who gave man the means to live in order and prosperity. The laws laid down for life in society materialized in the masks. So that when society is in danger of suffering the sorrows of the original world, men call upon the masks which, owing to their relationship with the gods, are able to reconcile the quarrels, subdue the witches, remove the evil forces, and re-establish order.

62
63    It is the alternation in movements and rhythm that char-
64 acterizes the zoua dance of the youth societies in the Guéré region. The young girls, brandishing scarves, move slowly at first and then quicken their pace, trying to impose their own rhythm on the drummers, who in turn try to regain the mastery of the rhythm of the dance.

*Bibliography*

B. Holas, *Les Masques kono*, Geuthner, Paris, 1952
H. Zemp, *Musique Dan*, Mouton, Paris, La Haye, 1971
E. Fischer, *Die Kunst der Dan*, Museum Rietberg, Zurich, 1976
R.J. Thompson, *African Art in Motion*, UCLA, Los Angeles, 1974

*Discography*

Recordings by Hugo Zemp:
*The Music of the Dan*, BM 30 L 2301
*Masques Dan*, OCR 52
*Musique Guéré*, LD 764

# The Central Guinea Coast

## Ivory Coast

### Guro (Zuénoula Region)

At the junction of two large groups, the Dan-Wobé-Guéré group to the west and the Baoule of Akan origin to the east, the Mandé-fu-speaking Guro have settled in a region of cultural and geographical transition. It is this transitional situation that accounts for their dynamic institutions.

Serious research has been carried out into the social and economic structure of this community, but their rituals, religion and representative symbols have scarcely been touched on. The ancestor cult and the funeral rites and other religious manifestations seem to be carried out in relation to the secret society, the guié.

The zamblé mask, which is a combination of antelope horns, 59 human face, big game jaws or toothed beak, is worn by a dancer whose gestures and lithe movements suggest the progress of the great antelope or the leopard.

*Discography*
*Musique Gouro de Côte-d'Ivoire*, OCR 48

### Baule (Yamoussoukro and Sakasou Region)

During the seventeenth century the kwa-speaking Baule migrated under the leadership of Aura Pokou, sister of the claimant to succeed the founder of the Ashanti kingdom. They reached the fertile savannah in the centre of what is now the Ivory Coast, and they form the most northerly advance post of the Akan branch.

This Akan origin and two centuries of contact with the neighbouring peoples have transformed the Baule society into a complex but original mixture of costumes and institutions.

The Baule are matrilineal, which means that the education of the children is undertaken by the mother's family and that all heritage is transmitted by the women. It also means that the chiefs hold their power from the female ancestors of the lineage. This accounts for the introduction of female masks into the enthroning ceremonies and any other demonstration of a chief's high rank. And these masks link the imagination of the community with their historical ancestress, Queen Aura Pokou.

These commemoration masks are presented together with the 65 insignia of high rank, such as the chief's staff, which is covered with gold leaf. The insignia are decorated with 'knots of wisdom' or animal effigies which symbolize the legal status of their holder.

In the Baule pantheon, Goli, son of Nyamié, the divinity of the sky, is the god who protects the village. He it is who is called upon during epidemics, invoked to threaten a woman guilty of adultery, implored to chase the evil spirits back to the bush. Goli, embodied in a mask representing a stylized buffalo head painted red and white, must be kept hidden from the sight of women.

The incarnation of Kakaguyé, spirit of the dead, has the power to make women barren. Therefore it is at night that he roams through the village, announcing his presence by jingling an iron bell and blowing on a horn carved from antelope horn, called the awé.

During the festivals, however, the mediators of Kakaguyé appear in a kindlier aspect. Gouli the red and Pondo Kakou the black, whose masks are a variation on that of Goli of the night, deliberately indulge in mockery and stigmatize everybody's failings.

Gouli and Pondo creep along in a crouching position, com- 66 pletely covered by two skirts of pineapple fibre and antelope hide. They are followed by a group of men, singing and shaking the towa, which is a resonator made from a calabash wrapped in a net to which are fixed cowries and beads. The rapid shaking of the instrument causes the shells and beads to beat on the resonator.

69
70 Every Baule village has one or two youth associations, who
71 try their strength in friendly dance contests. Sometimes members of these associations compete with each other by combining dance and music. The dancers, wearing short raffia skirts and indogo-coloured cotton pagnes, move to their own accompaniment of music, punctuating their movements with the rhythm of ankle bells and the beating of a laced hide drum.

---

*Discography*

*Musique baoulé-kodé*, OCR 34
*Pondo Kakou, musique de société secrète*, Vogue Lvlx 188

---

# Togo

## Ewé (or Évhé) (Keta Region)

The Ewé peoples from Toga and Ghana form a sort of cultural bridge between the Akan and the Yoruba. In fact, some of their institutions are comparable to those of the Ashanti to the west, while others resemble those of the Yoruba to the east. The Ewé claim ethnic unity in spite of the fact that since the beginning of the colonial era they have been split by an arbitrary border. In the photograph, the word ablodé, 'independence', is shown on the loin-cloth of one of their kings.

The Ewé group comprises about ten sub-groups, including the Ewé themselves, the Mina, the Anlo, and so on. Each of these sub-groups is divided into independent city-states, the du.

The du consists of about a hundred to a thousand people living in the political capital or in satellite villages. It is under the authority of a king, the fio, and of a council consisting of the elders of royal lineage, the chiefs of other clans and the military authorities.

When the presence of the fio and his council is required at a ceremony, strict rules of procedure are followed. Preceded by their own drums, the members of the high assembly arrive at the religious centre of the capital city. They are accompanied by their messenger, the sword-bearer aféna, and by the chancellor, who carries the gold-knobbed staff, the okyéamé poma. They seat themselves in accordance with their rank around the king,
73 whose arrival is announced by an orchestra of ivory trumpets.
72 The display of the regalia—head-dress, breastplates, gold

bracelets and necklaces—has a symbolic meaning. It confirms the authority and power of the fio and of his counsellors. To ensure the dual authority, at his enthronement the sovereign must swear never to jeopardize the unity of the du by refusing to submit to the approval of the assembly of elders.

The religious concepts of the Ewé are close to those of the Fon and of the Yoruba. Some of their religious creeds, including the voduwo yéwé (cult of thunder), the hébiéso (cult of lightning) and the afa (cult of divination) can be traced back to the vodun and to the orisha, practised to the east. The costume of the yéwé 74 priest, for example, which is made up of short superimposed loin-cloths evokes the vlaya of the Fon.

---

# Benin

(Abomey, Ouidah, Kétou and Savé Regions)

## 1. The Vodoun cults of the Fon

The vodoun cults concern various immaterial entities that act upon the universe. From the highly complex chart of interactions among divinities, ancestors and men, it can be concluded that for the Fon all human activity is linked to a whole body of forces which combine to perpetuate the man-god alliance. The gods receive their power from the homage paid to them by men, and men in turn achieve prosperity through the force of the gods.

Mahu and Lisa are the masters of all creation. The female element, Mahu, has the moon as emblem, while the sun is the emblem of Lisa, the male element. This couple is the origin of Dan, the rainbow snake who gave earth its form, and of Gu, the divinity of metal, and Hebioso—'so' meaning 'lightning'—the divinity of all celestial phenomena. Hebioso, as in the Yoruba shango, is the origin of all germination. It includes everything in the vodoun relating to lightning, thunder and rain, to running water, and even to 'standing water reflecting the sky'. Hebioso is represented by the sokpé, or lightning stones. It is also symbolized by the ordinary axe, or sossiovi, decorated by the fire-spitting ram or by the double bell, the kpanligan.

The Hebioso priests wear small vlaya skirts, and the rhythm of 75 their dance is rapid. Energetic movements of the body, impetuous whirlings and stampings, all express the fertilizing power of Hebioso.

Another cult is concerned with Dan, the principle of continuity. Its emblem is a snake biting its own tail. In this idea of continuity are included the notions of movement, of vital forces, of wealth and of recurrence.

Gu, the god of all metals, is the vodoun of the blacksmith, of 76 the warrior, of the peasants, and of all people who work with to 79 metal and use metal. The invoking of Gu may, however, be extended to all events that require his protection to deal with evil spirits. Gu is honoured through numerous animal sacrifices. The blood, a principle of life and thought, is the substantiation of the relationship between god and man. To confirm this alliance between the two worlds, the Fon use the term *e nu vodun*, 'to drink the vodoun'.

Hebioso, Dan and Gu are, so to speak, public vodouns. Tohosu, on the contrary, belong to the Abomey royal family cults, and they even have precedence in the rituals over the cults devoted to the creator couple. The 'Kings of the Water', originating from the deceased kings, have control over the destiny of their human subjects: they can restrain or they can encourage. This cult of the spirits of the deceased sovereigns is linked with the cult of Nésuhwé, the princely ancestors of the Abomey kings' families.

67
68 The priestesses of the Tohosu cult, clad in white robes and holding long staffs in their hands, perform three dances, each differing in rhythm, in front of the temple. These dances are called the ablo, the botro, and the nifossouso. During the ablo dance with its asoukablo rhythm, the 'princesses' advance in a sinuous line. Then they form a more compact group, waving their staffs like weapons, miming the passion of the warriors.

## 2. *Egungun and Gélédé*

The Yoruba culture, as expressed in Benin and in Nigeria, has two specific institutions: 'The Return of the Spirit of Death' and 'The Soothing of the Mothers'.

The Egun of deceased kings and heads of families comes down to earth in order to help man. He is represented by his children, the Egungun, who belong both to the world of the dead and to that of the living. They speak but are untouchable. Their
88 guardians, the mariwo, strike with their rods anyone who en-
89 deavours to approach them.
87 Their strange and magnificent costume is composed of a large rectangular-shaped head-dress with loose flaps, and of several long stoles which only partly hide the loin-cloth, sewn together at the ends. These strips of cloth are predominantly red, and are richly embroidered with masses of spangles and shells forming various chevron patterns. The edges of the stoles are always fringed. The abundance of decorative elements suggests power and wealth.

At the slightest movement, the cloth strips appear to come to life, and when the Egungun whirl around, 'a beneficial wind blows'.

Red is the colour that has the power to repulse evil spirits. The presence of the chevron patterns—the igbala—is a confirmation of the fact that the Egungun comes to 'save' man. The wind caused by the whirling movements brings security and promise of fortune. Finally, the crocodile representations on the breastplate are another proof of the power granted to the Egungun to help humankind.

The function of the Gélédé society is to appease the Mothers

and seek their help for the success of any undertaking: to give birth to beautiful children; to recover health; to grow fruitful harvest; to become rich.

The objective of the Gélédé society is to channel the specific power of women into a direction that is entirely conducive to the welfare of the group. The function of the masks is therefore 80 to evoke this beneficial image of the woman's role. There are to 86 numerous masks, both facial and also ventral or dorsal, and their 80 themes are fecundity and maternity. Others contain represen- 86 tations, of some delicacy, of familiar or picturesque themes. 81

When the nocturnal ceremonies for the 'Soothing of the to 84 Mothers' have taken place, and calm and order have returned, the Gélédé and ayoko, the clown masks, perched on stilts, 85 entertain the population. The enthusiasm thus evoked is linked up with the hope of once again seeing the Mothers approve of the plans of men.

---

*Bibliography*

P. Verger, *Dieux d'Afrique*, Hartmann, Paris, 1954
C. Savary, *Dahomey, traditions du peuple fon*, Musée d'ethnographie, Geneva, 1975
R. F. Thompson, *African Art in Motion*, UCLA, Los Angeles, 1974
U. Beier, Gélédé Masks' in *Odu*, Lagos, 1958

*Discography*

*Musiques dahoméennes*, OCR 17
*Musiques des Princes*, Vogue L VLX 192
*Musiques des Revenants*, Vogue EXTP 1026

---

# The Eastern Guinea Coast

## Cameroon

*Bamiléké and Bamun* (Bandjoun and Foumban Regions)

1. The elephant mask of the Bamiléké    90
to 98

At the head of the highly structured Bamiléké chiefdoms is a fon. He is assisted by a council composed of eight men, patrilineal descendants of the founders of the kingdom. The mkem, or assembly of the holders of hereditary rights, includes all the men who have rendered a great service to the kingdom; for example, war chiefs, or men who have enriched the royal treasury with elephant tusks or leopard skins. Each member of the mkem is head of a society with a specialized function: either religious, economic, military, and so on. The members of only two of these societies, the warrior societies of kuosi and kemdjé, are allowed to wear the elephant masks and the leopard skins. Ceremonies in which the wealth of the fon is displayed take place on the death of a fon or a man of high rank, or every two years, during the most important meetings of these societies.

Every item in the elephant mask costume denotes wealth, power and privilege. The multitude of glass beads which decorate it are ancient barter money, dating back to the slave-trade period. This display of wealth is in fact one of the functions of the mask. The elephant and the leopard are also evocative of force and power, both the power of the animals themselves, masters of the bush, and also that of the fon. For a fon is said to be able to transform himself into an elephant or a leopard. The long blue and white cotton coat, dyed 'in the reserve', is called the 'royal coat'.

100
101  On the nzo, one of the eight days in the Bamiléké week, the members of the Kemdjé society proceed, with faces veiled and holding the beaded leopard-headed staff, to transmit the fon's orders to the district chiefs. Similarly attired, they dance the nékang at various ceremonies, accompanied by the kué m'tong, who wear a feathered coat and a hat with horns.

102  2. *Bamun. The mbansié dance at Foumban*

103  This dance is performed by the warriors and soldiers of the sultan of Foumban's guard. Before paying the sultan homage, they mime a fight. The mbansié evokes the power of the sovereign's armies and can only take place in his presence. The orchestra is composed of drums and double bells.

*The bamun masks*

99  During official tours to Foumban, the masks of the sultan N'Joya are taken out of the Mosé Yépap room in the Bamun Museum of Art and Tradition, in order to be presented *in situ.*

---

*Bibliography*
R. Lecoq, *Les Bamileké,* Présence africaine, Paris, 1953
T. Northern, *The Sign of the Leopard,* University of Connecticut, Storrs, 1975

*Discography*
*Musique du Cameroun,* OCR 25
*Danses et Chants bamun,* SOR 3

---

2

3

5

7

6

8

9

14

15

3    16

19

20

21

25

26

27

33

37

38

39

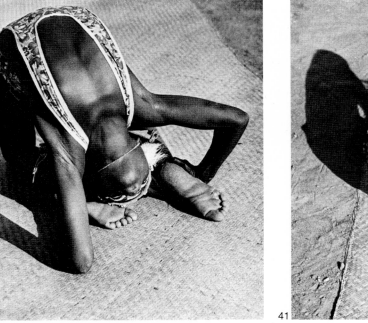

40

41

47

48

49

50

57

58

60

61

63

64

73

74

81

82

83

84

97

98

# WESTERN SUDAN

13: MALINKÉ
14: BAMANA
15: DOGON
16: KURUMBA
17: SAMO
18: BOBO
19: MOSSI
20: LOBI
21: SENOUFO
22: BORORO
23: MATAKAM
24: FALI
25: MASSA
26: MOUSSEY
27: SARA
28: DANGALÉAT

0        500        1000 km

# Western Sudan

## Western Sudan

### Guinea and Ivory Coast

*Malinké* (Kankan and Odienne Regions)

The Malinké date from the vast empire of Mali that spread over West Africa during medieval times. They became Moslems centuries ago.

It might be supposed that the adopting of the iconoclastic religion of Islam resulted in the wiping out of the indigenous culture, but in fact this was not the case. The Malinké of Upper Guinea, Mali and the north-western Ivory Coast have numerous cultural characteristics in common with their 'pagan' neighbours, the Senoufo or Bamana. Examples of these are the mask institution, initiation by age groups, the agrarian rituals, and socio-religious institutions such as the 'hunters', the 'musicians' the 'blacksmiths'.

The manykomori, like the komomanyaga of the Bamana, function as a sort of institutionalized self-criticism of society. The consequences of a too rigid enforcement of the marriage tradition, for example, may be satirized by the masks and the social roles played in one of these collective performances. The archetypal characters are involved in the scenario: the young
145 girl, the old husband, and the young lover. Komo, the great
146 mask to whom society attributes knowledge and wisdom, draws the moral of the play. Another sketch introduces a representative
149 of the hunter brotherhood. He wears a coat of feathers, several magic 'protectors' and a hood covered with cowries, and by his membership of a very ancient association he acts as a mediator in the conflicts of the farmers.
150 Lastly comes the monkey mask, akin to the koré mask of the
151 Bamana. This mask is a jester who enjoys with impunity the
152 privilege of using sarcasm to criticize society and point out its contradictions. It is a cultural mediator between man and animal, between man and woman, between neophyte and elders, and it has a privileged position as critic. Its ill-natured banter spares nobody: the doddering old marabout and the chief of the 'costumes', entangled in the rites, are both the butt of this mask's wit.

### Mali

*Bamana* (San and Bougouni Regions)

At the heart of the social and spiritual life of the Bamana lies an ideal of perfection. In order to reach the stage of fully matured adulthood, it is necessary to become a member of the six initiation societies (the Diow) in turn.

The last but one stage of this religious and moral teaching consists of the initiation into the tyiwara.

Cultivating the savannah in this central region of Mali is very hard work for the farming population, and their efforts are frequently jeopardized by climatic conditions. The symbolic representations of the vital Earth-Man relationship has given rise to numerous myths and to intense ritual activity. It is in the heart of the tyiwara that the legends, beliefs and truths concerning the Man-Universe relationship are revealed.

The following is a summary of the myth of the one who gave his name to this initiation society, a myth that works by analogy and similarity. At the beginning of the world, a being that was both animal and human, child of Mousso Koroni and of a snake, taught the people, with the aid of his staff and his claws, how to change the thorny bush into millet fields. The Bamana who followed his example became happy and prosperous. But the abundance of good things caused them to become careless of the Earth and forgetful of the tributes owed to the one who had brought the knowledge of agricultural techniques. Tyiwara reacted to this ingratitude by burying himself deep in the earth and waiting for men to redeem themselves and render to him the homage he deserved. Thereupon they sculpted antelope effigies (sogoni kun) and took them to the fields when the millet was being hoed in order to honour the memory of the Bamana benefactor.

The richness of the soil and consequently the survival of the group therefore depend on the intervention of the members of the tyiwara society. These members usually go in couples, concealing themselves under a mud-dyed fibre cloak and leaning on a burrowing staff. Their heads are covered with a basketwork cap on which is fixed the stylized representation of a male antelope (hippotrague or orycterope) or of a female antelope (oryx or kob). Occasionally, and usually in the
120 Bougouni region, a female statuette evoking Mousso Koroni, the mother of Tyiwara, is associated with the antelope.
121 The female antelope, the Earth, whose high, upright and
122 rigid horns symbolize the growing of the seeds in the damp soil,
123 is also the Mother of mankind, as represented by the fawn she bears on her back. Above the fawn, the male hippotrague with its full flowing mane is suggestive of the sun whose warmth fertilizes the earth. The chevron pattern round his neck symbolizes the Bamanan concept of the zig-zag course followed by the sun.

Vernacular interpretations of tyiwara sculptures are far removed from the somewhat stereotyped image of African art that they often seem to present to Western eyes.

*Bibliography*

D. Zahan, *Sociétés d'initiation bambara*, Mouton, Paris-La-Haye, 1960
P. J. Imperato, "The Dance of the Tyiwara", *African Arts*, vol. IV, No. 1, Los Angeles, 1971

*Dogon* (Sangha Region)

In Dogon territory, the period between the death of a man and the end of the mourning ceremonies which close the funeral cycle is quite a long one. If the deceased had held an important social or religious position, or had attended the Sigui sixtieth birthday ceremonies either in his own village or in a neighbouring region, then after the 'first funeral' the family will accumulate goods that can be exchanged to enable them to organize a dance. This ritual preparation period for the 'departure of the deceased man's soul' is considered dangerous for the deceased's own family and, by extension, the whole village. Numerous taboos are therefore enforced on them, while the homeless soul roams through the village, haunting the various places he once frequented.

The function of the dama, apart from raising the taboos, is to master this secret force that emanates from the deceased and direct it through the medium of masks to the sacred places where it will in some way or another be fixed. At the end of the dama the deceased will belong to the ranks of ancestors. It is through them that the word of Amma, the Creator, will be transmitted again in all its vital force to mankind, fertilizing the fields and making fecund the women and the cattle.

This recreation of an order that has been disturbed by death
115 involves a wide display of symbolic practices: the deploying of
to 119 masks, songs, music and an abundant consumption of food and millet beer. Sometimes the dama may last as long as six days.

The beginning of the dama preparations is announced by the sound of the rhombe, which is a wooden or metal saw-edged plate whirled round at the end of a rope by one of the initiates. The humming sound of this instrument is regarded as the voice of the very first ancestor.

From that moment, the circumcised members of the Awa—a mask society—repaint or carve afresh the masks that they will wear. This takes place away from the village, in rocky shelters or in the bush. The hoods and the short skirts for the costumes are made from the bark of the pollo tree, and the long skirts from sanseviera fibres. These are plaited and dyed black, red or yellow. Cowries and various other ornaments are fixed to the hoods and the breastplates.

When the masks emerge from the secret places where they have been fashioned, their arrival is announced in the village and the women and children take shelter in their huts, since the members of the Awa are not indulging in a gay masquerade. They are actors in a cosmic theatre, aiming to recreate the creation of the world, of men, of vegetable and animal species, and of the stars. What is happening is that this period of danger and disorder that has been brought about by the death is now brought to an end by the evocation of the fundamental moments in the genesis of the universe. The audience, enthusiastic but solemn, watches with great attention the development of the different stages in the ritual.

At the dama of a spiritual chief or a village notable, the place where the sacred dances are held is invaded by an impressive number of different masks. Of these the most numerous and the most symbolic are the kanaga and the sirigé masks.

The kanaga is topped by a short pole to which two parallel 117 blades are fixed perpendicularly. Two small flat boards are placed at their ends, upwards for the upper blade, downwards for the lower blade. The face of the mask is partly encircled by a crest of very stiff fibres, dyed either red or yellow.

To the uninitiated, this mask evokes a bird spreading its wings. For those who have attained analogical knowledge through initiation, it is the symbol of man, axis of the world, pointing to both earth and sky. Another interpretation links kanaga to the water insect which, at the birth of the world, implanted in the soil the first seed from which all other seeds and all human archetypes sprung. And the flat, crushed shape of the pole of kanaga evokes the fall of the first trouble-maker, Ogo, the pale fox.

All these variations are included in one of the figures of the dance. The dancer, with a rapid movement of the upper part of the body, sweeps the mask close to the ground, thus evoking the internal vibration that animates the matter created for Amma.

The sirigé mask has a rectangular face divided by a vertical 118 ridge with two hollowed spaces. It is topped by a huge blade, sometimes nearly fifteen feet high. This blade, which is alternately painted and pierced, shows patterns of parallel lines and opposing triangles. Sirigé means 'storied house', and several meanings are concentrated into this term. There are the different stages of creation, the degrees severing the earth from the sky, the curve of the arch, the genetic sequence and also, in the vertical parallel lines, the frontage of the ginna or 'family house', representing by analogy the vast human family.

After a few steps, and following a rapid change in the drum rhythm, the sirigé mask-wearer kneels towards the east. Then he moves the top of his body backwards and forwards, forcing the extreme end of the blade to touch the ground, and thus marking the limits of the horizon and the cardinal points. As he raises himself up, he creates whirling horizontal motions 119 with the mask which suggest the evolution of the sun around the earth, analogous to the universe being created by the rotation of the divine axis.

Kanaga and sirigé are followed by masks that are more 116 familiar to the uninitiated, since they are made in accordance with a less abstract concept. These masks evoke the behaviour of some of the animals that haunt this part of the bush, encompassed by a loop in the River Niger. They include, among others, antelopes, hares, lions and monkeys. Other masks mime the behaviour of various Dogon social characters. There is the 'old man' mask, the young girl, with a face made from cowries 115 and breasts of baobab fruits, the 'ritual thief', and the masks of caste such as the 'blacksmith', the 'shoe-maker', and so on. Foreigners, too, are represented in this vast pageantry. There is the mask of the 'Peul woman', characterized by the head-dress peculiar to this ethnic group; the mask of the 'Bamana woman', and others. Sometimes there is even the 'Missus', or white woman mask, and that of the 'Dokotor', the ethnographer.

*Bibliography*

M. Griaule, *Masques dogon,* Institut d'ethnologie, Paris, 1938
J. Laude, *African Art of the Dogon,* Viking Press, New York, 1973

*Discography*

*Les Dogon,* OCR 33, Ocora
*Scènes de la vie des Dogon,* Resonance No.3

## Upper Volta

*Kurumba* (Aribinda Region)

The Kurumba, who live on the borders of Upper Volta and Mali, are said to have been chased from their native territory further to the north by the Dogon invaders They migrated to the Yatenga district in the Lurum region, where they have been settled since the sixteenth century. Recent studies by Dutch archaeologists and anthropologists have, however, challenged this long-held thesis.

The Nioniosi, as the Kurumba call themselves, are grouped into several clans: the Sawadougou, the Oueremi, the Zalé, the Tao, and so on. They use a cultural material consisting mainly of steles, forks and masks. This material is designed to establish a relationship between the etiological elements of the myth and the cyclical or historical events of funeral or agrarian rituals.

113 The adone, sculptures depicting antelopes, are mostly shown
114 at the ceremonies marking the end of the mourning for a 'land chief'. The wandering spirit of the deceased, his shadow, is captured by the adone, and is thus made temporarily into the seat of the altar.

The polychrome antelopes seem to be the property of the Sawadougou clan, and the sculptors and wearers of the adone are recruited exclusively from this family. This privilege re-inforces the religious power of the Sawadougou, who are regarded as the direct descendants of the founder-ancestors of the Nioniosi society.

According to the original myth, Sawadougou, the civilizing hero, is said to have descended from the sky wearing a mask. His wife and children, who accompanied him, were endowed
113/114 with the features of the antelope, the hyena and the hare.

*Bibliography*

A. M. Schweeger-Hefel, 'L'art nioniosi', *Journal de la Société des africanistes,* Vol.XXXVI, No.2, Paris, 1966

*Samo* (Kiembara Region)

Two complementary groups are responsible for the religious life of the Samo village communities of the Yatenga region: the 'rain people' and the 'earth people'.

The earth people are concerned with all rituals dealing with death and ancestors and are in charge of the funeral rites. The
155 rain people deal with the agrarian rites. They form male initiation
156 associations and at the end of the dry season they organize all the rituals required to bring forth rain.

The costumes and head-dresses are covered with a mass of cowries. On the crest is a sun symbol, and the music is a rattling of bolts and rings on the metallic resonators. All these are symbolic of the prosperity and abundance that will come if the celestial phenomena prove favourable.

The cowries, in particular, symbolize the prosperous future that the rain will bring, for these cowries are both barter money and magic objects conducive to fertility and fecundity.

*Bobo* (Bouni, Koumi and Dédougou Regions)

The generic term 'Bobo' is usually applied to those people living in an area bounded on the north by Djenné in Mali, on the east by the Ghanaian border, on the south by Bobo-Dioulasso, and by the upper region of the Bani river to the west.

The name was given long ago by the Manding invaders and various qualifying adjectives were added to it: Fing (black) for the southern natives, Oulé (red) for those of the San and Dedougou regions, and Die (white) for those of Hounde and neighbouring villages.

These three sub-groups are not united under the sovereignty of one chief, but the Bobo people are divided into as many autonomous political and economic units as there are villages. All these little groups, however, appear to share the same concept of the relationship between man and nature, both from the symbolic and from the practical point of view.

In these regions agriculture is the predominant source of wealth. The fear of drought or even a delay in the arrival of the rainy season are a source of great mental distress, and to ease this distress the farmers of the dry savannah have conceived an elaborate scheme of institutions and rites that preserve the relationship between man and earth, the source of all life and survival. The Bobo differ from other societies in that they do not represent nature as an ambivalent force. Nature is not at the same time both generous and dangerous, but appears as essentially benevolent. It is the mistakes and offences of mankind that upset her, and also man's needs. So the function of the masks is to chase away the evil that is bound to spring up in human communities. This purification role, which is indispensable to the cyclical renewal of vegetation, is directly linked to the creation myth.

Wuro the creator installed a harmonious order between the sun, the rain and the earth. But man, owing to his way of life as well as to his weaknesses, threatened this equilibrium. The techniques of agriculture involve a violation of the soil which outraged Soxo, the divinity of the bush and, through him, Wuro the creator. In addition to this, transgressing the laws of society have an effect on the natural environment. Breaking of a taboo could bring about a sequence of calamities in both the natural and the human sphere. Drought leads to starvation, sickness, sterility and sometimes to death. But Wuro the creator gave some of his bounty to Dwo, whose function is to act as mediator between man and God and to restore the initial equilibrium when it has been menaced.

170
171 Dwo is primarily incarnated in the 'leaf masks'. These, though essentially primitive, are nevertheless of great importance.

The Fing call them koro, the Oulé call them siriuréoro, and they are made in the bush after the millet crop has been safely stored. The leaves used are those of the karité, or bastard mahogany tree. They are tied together with vegetable fibre and completely cover the body of the wearer. The presence of a feather or straw crest, the zami, indicates that the mask is male.
170 Sometimes a basketwork cone provides for an enlarged opening at face level.

The leaf masks enter the village at dusk. They roam through the alleys, lightly brushing against store-houses, huts and the people of the village. The rustling leaves 'shoulder' all the 'dust particles' representing the offences of mankind. They 'wash' them, so to speak, of all the impurities that stain them, thus absorbing into themselves all the evil that has accumulated during the year.

The ceremonies designed to regenerate the human community by participating in the renewal rites of nature take place at the end of the dry season, before the first rain falls and agricultural work is taken up again.

These rites signify the end of the period of mourning, purification and the supplication of chthonian forces. They require the presence of the leaf masks and also of the fibre and sculptured masks.

The fibre masks are plaited and dyed by the blacksmiths, and because of their use of natural materials, they are associated with the entities of the bush. But they also include elements relating to man, such as the geometrical patterns around the
168 crest that are, in fact, the armorial drawings of a clan. They

therefore form a transitional element between the leaf masks 169 and the sculptured masks. These latter are usually in animal forms 164 and they represent the protective genii of the village. They include the warthog, the male flat-horned buffalo, the female buffalo with circularly sectioned horns, the cock with its crest perpendicular to the face, the toucan, the fish, the antelope, the 162 serpent, which is sometimes as much as ten feet long, and lastly 165 the butterfly, whose fluttering movements after the first rains 166 are imitated by the mask wearer. 167

Another type of mask of Gurunsi origin is the doyo or nwo. This has a round face and eyes in concentric circles and it is topped by a polychrome blade. It combines such animal motifs as an owl face, a caloo beak, and sometimes a 'snake skeleton', with geometrical patterns such as lozenges, checks, opposing triangles and chevron.

Whether made of leaf, fibre or wood, whether realistic or abstract, all these masks embody the benevolent force of Dwo and therefore the concept of fertility, fecundity and growth.

Anthropomorphous masks are rare because, according to Bobo philosophy, man's survival depends on receiving the gifts of Dwo, and in order to receive this beneficence, man must renounce his own arrogance.

---

*Bibliography*
Guy Le Moal, 'Rites de purification et d'expiation', *Systèmes de signes*, Hermann, Paris, 1978

---

*Mossi* (Koudougou Region)

The 'red dancers' of Koudougou belong to a sect of former 160 captives of Gurunsi origin. 161

At one time they were servants of a traditional Mossi chief, the Moogo Naaba of Ouagadougou. It was their duty to look after their master's horses and they are still sometimes called the 'red horsemen'.

The colour of their costume is the same colour as the saddle blanket of the king's horse. The horse-tail fly whisk recalls their former office as stable boys and their dance movements evoke the leaping of the horse.

Nowadays the dancers wear a crested head-dress, but at one time they would wear a calabash for a period of nine years in order to ensure long life for their land chief, Tengsoba.

*Lobi* (Gaona Region)

The Lobi farmer-hunters inhabit the region where the three lands of Upper Volta, Ghana and Ivory Coast meet. Their dances are not merely an entertainment to accompany their rites, but have a deep inner meaning. They are designed to express in movement the very rhythm of the universe, the very essence of energy, the divine force that animates the world.

153
154
This dynamic principle of vital force can be seen in the choreography of the initiation dances at Dyoro or Bur, which are performed during the dry season to give thanks to the divinities of the bush for having shown favour towards the crops.

In order to evoke this concept the dances progress in a spiral that spreads out from a central point where the orchestra is based.

## Ivory Coast

*Senoufo* (Sinematiali, Boundiali and Korhogo Regions)

All religious, social, economic and political activities in the Senoufo territory are bound up in some way or other with the complex institution called the Poro. All members of the group, with the exception of blacksmiths and former captives, acquire their knowledge of the rules of community life within the structure of the Poro.

The creation myth explains the predominance of the Poro. In the beginning the world had neither structure nor laws, and humanity was therefore unable to organize itself into society. Kulotyolo, the creator god, helped this embryo of humanity by laying down a set of basic laws to regulate the first cosmic phenomena. But he soon wearied of his efforts to help his human offspring, and the threat of a return to universal chaos therefore hangs perpetually over the world. Children, for example, are imperfect beings, and there is a risk that the original chaos could be reactivated by them. Then there are the witches, vehicles for evil forces and confusion, who secretly undermine the frail institutional system. Lastly there is sickness and death, which in the Senoufo mind are seldom connected with natural causes, but are regarded as manifestations of the destructive and negative principle present in the universe. In the face of dangers such as these, it is considered essential that the forces of creation should be constantly strengthened so that every generation re-creates, symbolically, both man and human society. This is the main function of the Poro. Before he turned into a remote being, neglectful of his offspring, the creator had transferred part of his organizing power to a spirit living in a sacred grove, the Sinzanga, not far from the village. This supernatural being is called Kaatyeleo, 'ancient mother of the village'. She is aware of the misfortunes of men, and it is she who gives her force and energy to the Poro. She is the mother at its centre. It is in the sacred grove, in her bosom, that the men accomplish the final stage of their initiation.

But before describing the ceremonies in which the Senoufo males undergo the final ordeals before reaching full maturity,
140
to 144
let is look at the kagba ritual in which the giant ox Nasolo (literally, 'elephant-ox') is presented to the neophytes. This

unique being, Nasolo, moves around the periphery of the central Sinzanga accompanied by a guide-interpreter, Kodalu, who is completely covered by a cotton garment. They appear to be moving rather at random, but in fact Nasolo moves with great precision from one demarcated plot to the other, all along the sacred grove.

Nasolo consists of a light wooden cylindrical frame covered with braid and decorated with geometrical patterns in many different colours. Kagba means, in fact, 'many-coloured'. In front is a sculptured head combining antelope and crocodile motifs, and sometimes elements of man. At the back is a tail of plaited raffia. The whole structure is often well over a metre in height and sometimes as much as five metres in length. It is manoeuvred by two men hidden inside. Sometimes one of the bearers manipulates a sort of rubbing device that emits a sound resembling a lion's roar. For the neophytes, although the elements are not homogeneous and do not recall any specific creature, Nasolo represents a buffalo, symbol of intellectual and physical perfection. The apprenticeship of the neophytes ends with the initiation into this analogical method of thought, which correlates Nasolo with Tyolobélé, the fully initiated adult.

The final stage of adult initiation into the Poro takes place during the full moon of December. The future Tyolobélé wait naked at the edge of the sacred grove. Then a hand, whose owner is not visible in the obscurity, firmly grasps each candidate and takes him into the lair of Kaatyeleo, mother of the Poro. There follow various purification ordeals, after which the candidate has to crawl along a muddy tunnel which leads to the sacred enclosure. The symbolism of this act is plain enough: man returns to his mother's womb. This return to the bosom of Kaatyeleo is accompanied by a rattling sound and by the howling of the Poro dignitaries, who remain invisible in the night. The rattling is the agony of the old man dying to make way for the new-born, and the howling is the wailing of a new-born child.

126
127
One by one those who have become initiates of Tyolo by means of this second birth put on the clothes and ornaments indicative of their newly acquired status and leave the Sinzanga and move towards the village, where they will be received with great jubilation.

The villagers are delighted to see this new generation of men who will guarantee their safety and protect them against any assault that comes out of the bush, and they show their gratitude in the end-of-initiation ceremonies, or kafo.

129
130
124
125
132
The Tyolobélé are joined by a variety of characters, equally representative of the power of the Poro. These include the Nayogo, who wear huge crests decorated with cowries; the Kwonbélé, who have heads topped by multi-coloured wooden helmets; the Fré, whose brown-speckled costumes show that they are the panthers of the Poro; and lastly the Poniugo masks, meaning, literally, 'Poro heads'.

Women are also initiated, although their rites differ from those

104

of the men. The male Poro does not include the ordeal of circumcision at the first stage of initiation, but that of the women
133 does involve excision at this stage. The woman's kafo, although
134 less frequent, is quite as spectacular as the man's. Numerous dances take place, and sumptuous costumes, decorated with multitudes of shells, are worn.

The complexity of the Senoufo funeral rites derives both from the importance of the event and from the danger incurred by the whole group. The spirit of the dead man roams around the village and lingers in the spots he used to frequent. If this force is allowed to roam freely around, it could bring back the original chaos. It is therefore essential that it should be captured. The initiates alone have the power and energy to overcome the dead man's spirit.

136 The Tyolobélé blow on great horns made out of a single piece of wood. These are the nanaa, and they evoke the roar of a
138 lion. The Poro dignitaries beat on thin, high-pitched drums called tyepingdaana. They are accompanied by the laladyogo, an enigmatic character muffled up in a cotton cloth which reveals
136 only the eyes. On his head he wears a large plaited straw hat decorated with the white and black feathers of a fishing eagle. Finally, the Poro masks join the procession. Among them are the
135 gpeligé masks with their tyobigé drums, and the alarming
139 Waniugo.

The strange procession follows the tracks of the dead man's soul through the village and up to the bed on which his body lies. One of the gpeligé masks then takes a small armpit drum, jumps up on the bed and stands astride the corpse, all the time beating a rapid tattoo on the instrument with his fingers. He is assisted by an initiate who shakes iron bells to the same rhythm. The function of this ritual is to stress, with the help of the music, the power of the Poro, and also to chase the dead man's soul right away from the village and the cultivated fields and into the region of the dead.

## Nigeria

*Peul Bororo* (Dakoro Region)

The various studies devoted to the pastoral nomads of the Sahel region, whether economic, technological, or more generally anthropological, all agree on one essential element of the culture of the Peul of the bush, and that element is, their great concern for beauty.

The gerewol institution, which many observers have called 'a real beauty contest', has been frequently described. The celebration of an aesthetic ideal by means of cosmetics, ornaments, dance and song, is not, however, limited to this annual ceremony. It would appear that all the cultural manifestations characteristic of this society are focused on the idea of beauty.

For the Bororo, beauty, freedom and happiness are linked together. In effect, to live in freedom and happiness means to roam, unhampered by any permanent ties, through the beautiful scenes of unspoilt nature; to amble at the pace of cattle, following the beautiful Bororooji zebu with their heavy horns and mahogany-coloured hides. It also means producing a numerous progeny of beautiful young boys and girls. And finally, it means keeping up traditions. The opposite to all this is sorrow and ugliness, which are the marks of the settled life. When parasite diseases threaten the herd, when the pasture lands progressively dry up, and when the average age of the men dramatically increases, then the Bororo fear that they will be forced to bring to an end their seasonal moving of livestock from one region to another. To remain settled in one spot means losing the Peul way of life. It means losing the ethnic unity of the lineage through cross-breeding; it means losing one's singularity, the will to be different. To cultivate the land is to lose one's horizons.

During the dry season, however, they are obliged to make a temporary halt around the permanent water-holes in Southern Niger and Northern Nigeria. This enforced stop is compensated for by a series of ceremonial and exchange activities that serve to reaffirm alliances between the groups. The gerewol and a few weddings take place during this period, and there are also meetings called the 'market' which take place on the outskirts of the camp between members of the same age groups.

At the end of the afternoon or at dusk the unmarried men of 107 different lineages put on their most beautiful loin-cloth over to 112 their leather trousers. Their faces are dyed yellow ochre, their lips are blackened with indigo. With their sword fixed to their belt, and sometimes holding an axe-stick (jalel) or spear, they place themselves in a line, elbow to elbow, in accordance with a strict order. The guests are to the south, the hosts to the north, the eldest in the middle, and the youngest at each end.

The yaké is danced slowly with knees bent, one foot over the 108 other, and hands clapping. This linear dance is performed in two stages. In the first stage the dancers face each other, and in the second they make a quarter turn with the body and step to the side. The movements appear to be restrained, and the alternating 107 stamping and jumping are performed without exuberance. There is a fixed expression on the face: mouth smiling broadly to disclose the beauty of the teeth, eyes wide open to show the whiteness of the eyeballs.

Before the yaké, as before the gerewol, the men drink a beverage made from red honey, milk, red ficus and ground gypse. The components of this drink possess the qualities of colour and charm which are to be transferred to the dancers.

The young girls, also from different lineages, encircle the group. They clap their hands and make their metal ornaments tinkle. At the end of the yaké one or two of the girls move 109 forward to pick out those whom they consider the most hand- to 112 some. Those who have been chosen leave the line and throw their jalel up in the air.

The social function of the yaké is obvious. It is intended to encourage alliances between different lineages on the basis of aesthetic judgements. If a man is handsome then he can only be a good man, careful of the traditions of the Bororo.

*Bibliography*

M. Dupire, *Peul nomades,* Institut d'ethnologie, Paris, 1962.
J. Delange, 'Les Peul', *Cahiers d'études africaines,* vol. IV, No. 1, Paris, 1963

# Central Sudan

## Cameroon

### Matakam (Oudjula Region)

172
to 176 The Matakam tribes live in the North Cameroon in the Mandara mountains. Their funeral rites and harvest festivals are celebrated at the same time as the commemoration of those who have died during the year, and numerous dances, both of men and of women, are involved. The actual forms of these ceremonies have been described with great accuracy, but the observers appear to have overlooked the significance that these dances hold for the community itself.

The dance of the 'men at arms', bearing shield, assegai and bow, draws to a close with the hurling of a spear on to the dead man's roof, a symbolic gesture which is carried out by the eldest son of the deceased. This is rather surprising when taken in conjunction with the other activities of the group, which consist of various sacrifices and ritual libations intended to honour the dead man's memory.

Closely allied to the warlike dance of the men is that of the women, who brandish a small sickle for this purely ceremonial purpose.

One may tentatively put forward the hypothesis that this paroxysmal display of energy is meant to compensate for that loss of the breath of life that has been brought about by death.

### Fali (Bossoum Region)

177
to 179 It is the women who have the privilege of symbolically feeding the dead with offerings of gruel and millet beer during the Fali funeral rites. And similarly, during the leuru beleng, the yearly homage paid to the ancestor, the women from every clan in the village will come in procession with a calabash of millet beer to be poured over the gaw lasindji stones where the dead man's breath of life has settled.

### Massa (Yagoua Region)

At certain times of year, either between October and February or between January and June, the Massa men aged between eighteen and thirty whose families have not recently been affected by a death, abandon their daily activities and obligations and assemble in groups of ten to forty in camps where they will practise gourou, that is, a 'milk cure'.

Each guruna takes with him a few choice cows which either belong to his own family or have been left to his care by the chief of the enclosure to whom he is subordinate. When they are in the camp, the guruna will care jointly for the cattle and will consume not only the milk, but also the plentiful supply of meat, cakes and sorghum gruel brought to them by the neighbouring village people. Above all they will learn the different wrestling holds (nafta) and the songs and dances (liuta) that they will perform publicly at funeral ceremonies or 192 on other occasions when they can excite admiration.

During the whole gourou period they are exempt from the punishments that are normally imposed by the community on those breaking the rules—punishment for theft, adultery, insults and gluttony, for example. The performance of the guruna, their display of physical strength and their quality as dancers or fighters, establishes the prestige of the family group to which they belong and ensures that rivals or future allies will recognize its prosperity. The guruna do not, in general, take part in sacred affairs, but the powers of transgression bestowed on them may be used for ritual purposes to banish symbolically dangers that may come from the outside world. Thus, when adorned with the bird-headed crest, the guruna has the power to 193 chase all malevolent entities back into the bush. 194

## Chad

### Moussey (Gounou-Gaya Region)

Among the Moussey who live in the south-east of Chad in the Gounou-Gaya region, one of the chief manifestations of the 186 spiritual life is to be found in the possession cult. 187

If a member of the community, either male or female, 188 appears to be disturbed either in bodily functioning or in social behaviour, then he or she abandons all normal activities and joins the fulina group.

There, cared for by his initiators, he will learn by means of dreams and trances to identify the spirit that is inhabiting him and to name it. From that moment, delivered of his torments, he will appease the spirit that dwells within him with sacrificial offerings. He becomes a priest of the cult of the genie that has 'ridden' him and takes part in the different ritual celebrations where his presence is required. Thus during the rain supplication 188 rites the priest of the earth, host of Fulloma, as indicated by the

blue, white and black beads on his necklace, swings calabashes
187 over the head of a woman 'possessed' by the genie of Death,
Fulmatna (red beads). This symbolic gesture is meant to establish an accord between the two spirits so that they will grant the prayer of man for rain.

### Sara (Maro and Bedaya Regions)

201 In addition to the bamboo whistle (nal) and the eight-chord bowed harp (kendé), there are three other musical instruments in the Sara orchestra: the kod kirgoutou, a cylindrical drum with two laced hides; the gangué, a slim long vertical hand-beaten drum with a pegged hide; and the koundou, a portable xylophone with a calabash sound-box. The semi-circular frame of this last instrument is fixed to the musician's waist, so that he can play standing up. The fourteen or fifteen bars are struck with small
180 hammers whose ends are fitted with latex balls.
185    The female initiation rites, the Ndo Banan, end with song and
to 189 dance. The heads of the young girls are completely shaved; their faces are veiled by a bead 'mask'; they wear long necklaces down to their busts, several copper bracelets on their forearms, and a belt of iron bells. The Ndo Banan is divided into two parts. First, the singing part, where the chorus of initiatory mothers alternates with the chorus of the young initiates. Second, the dance, where the energetic movement of the hips causes the iron bells to sound a rhythm closely following the rhythmic beat of the calabash drums.

The Sara initiation involves the death of the child to his intimate family and his rebirth as a member of the community. To mark this loss of their original identity, the boys wear a leaf mask and the girls a mask of beads. Where the arable land belongs to the male members of the clan, the instruments necessary to turn agricultural products into consumable food are the exclusive property of the women, and this is stressed by the display of earthenware dishes at the final initiation dance.
184 After initiation, girls and boys of similar age groups perform
185 dances whose function is to show their full membership of
189 society. The body markings, tattoos and scarifications are
191 evidence of this, But these ritual encounters are also aimed at encouraging future alliances between members of opposing lineages.

*Bibliography*
Robert Jaulin, *La Mort Sara*, 10/18 UGE, Paris, 1971

*Discography*
*Anthologie de la musique du Tchad*, OCR 36

### Dangaleat (Korbo Region)

In the vast mountain range in the centre of Chad live several groups of different ethnic origin and dialect. These people 'driven back' from the mountains are known under the generic term of Hadjeray.

If for administrative reasons the villages have been regrouped in the plains, the places where they practise their cults still remain in the 'mountains'. The Dangaleat from the Korbo region, like their neighbours the Diongor and the Kenga, believe in the existence of Margaï, a sort of genie of the place who lives in the heights overlooking the houses and the granaries. For these peanut and millet farmers the help of the Margaï is essential if good crops are to be ensured, if they are to be protected from natural disasters such as drought and tornados, and also to maintain the physical and cultural entity of the group.

So the end of the crop harvesting is an occasion for great 197
rejoicing, when sacrifices are made to the spirits of the 'high 198
places', and dances of possession by the benevolent power of 199
the Margaï will be performed over a period of several days. 200

107

124

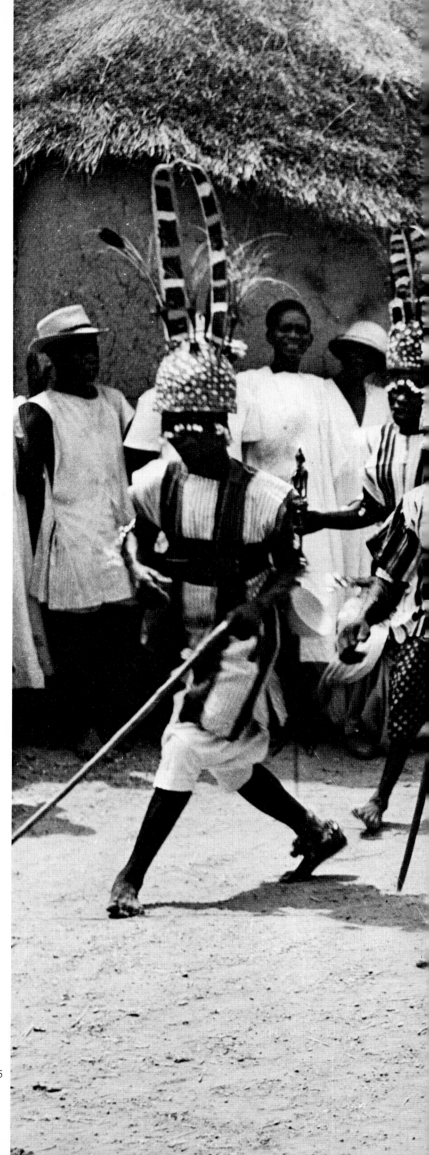

125

136

137

138

147

174

177

178

179

186

187

191

92

# EQUATORIAL
# AFRICA

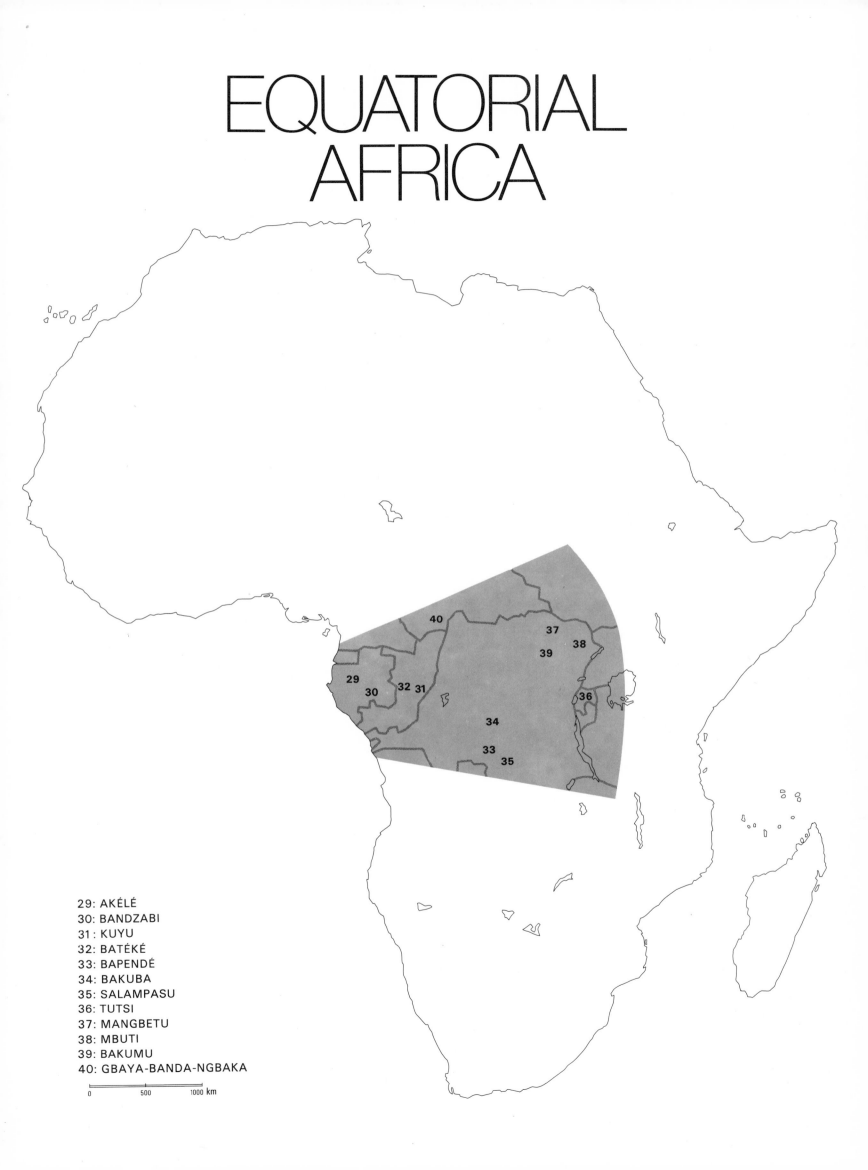

29: AKÉLÉ
30: BANDZABI
31 : KUYU
32: BATÉKÉ
33: BAPENDÉ
34: BAKUBA
35: SALAMPASU
36: TUTSI
37: MANGBETU
38: MBUTI
39: BAKUMU
40: GBAYA-BANDA-NGBAKA

0       500      1000 km

# Equatorial Africa

## The Ogowe Basin

### Gabon

#### Akélé (Ndjolé Region)

The Bwiti initiation cult is not specific to the Akélé, but like other communities they took it over from the Mitsogho. This syncretic institution has absorbed features from various cultures, and its origins may well lie in the religious practices of the trade slaves from the east. The Mitsogho gave it a liturgical language and a framework for its expression, that of the ancestor cult. The Bwiti has superimposed itself on other ritual manifestations and sometimes even replaced them, and it has left a deep mark on the religious and social life of many of the ethnic groups in Gabon.

Quite a number of its adherents were repressed by the colonial Civil Service, which believed that the extension of this cult could result in a challenge to their own authority. Missionaries, persuaded that it represented a revival of fetishism, urged the destruction of the temples and of the sculptured effigies used in the cult. The traditional structures of the Bwiti therefore came under attack from two sides: from the Europeans who controlled the political systems and from the intensive penetration of the great world religions. Had it not been for the rival factions, the Bwiti would have given way to the establishment of a cultural, political and social consensus. But because the members of the Bwiti were obliged to go underground and carry out their rites in small groups and in secret, these rites adapted themselves to the different ethnic settings. There are variations between these different groups—some of them exclude women, for instance, and others admit the presence of women—but certain of the features of the sect are to be found
222 in more than one group. One such feature is the 'men's house', the ebandza, which is the sacred place of the cult. A fire burns perpetually in its centre, and the flickering shadows of its flames bring to life the walls made of decorated bark. In the middle of the open façade there is a supporting pole, the éengo, which has a sculpture of the female form or else a lozenge pattern that symbolizes the female sex. The sense of universal mystery is transmitted to the community of adherents by the reciting of myths, and by songs and music, with the ngombi bowed harp stressing the most important 'words'. Chewing the hallucinogenic bark of the iboga helps to stimulate euphoria, and the supernatural world of the ancestors is revealed to the members of the sect.

Strengthened by this cosmic vision they are then able to
220 perform the dangerous 'flame dance' around the sacred pole and
221 round the periphery of the ebandza.

*Discography*
*Gabon: Musique des Mitsogho et des Batéké*, OCR 84

#### Bandzabi (Mbigou Region)

The daylight outings of the Bandzabi masks with stilts are 215 symbolic expressions of the ambiguous relationship that exists to 219 between the world of the living and the world of the dead. Bandzabi society seeks to mitigate the anxiety of death by a greater familiarity with it, but on the other hand the ancestors must not be completely identified with their descendants.

These masks have been observed to arouse ambivalent feelings in their audience, particularly in the women and children. There is a mixture of respect, fear and defiance, and sometimes abuse is hurled at the masks.

This attitude may be explained by the following three factors: First, the appearance of the mask recalls the group's ideal of 215 feminine beauty. On earth, as in the hereafter, the criteria for such beauty are the same. A wide, clear-cut face, with lozenge-shaped scarifications, each containing nine red points both in the front of the face and on the temples; slanting eyes, and a harmonious arrangement of braids. Second, the stark white face evokes the chilling beauty of 'the girl from the land of the dead'. And third, the phantom-like effigy swaying on its stilts as if 216 caught between two worlds, is an enigma to the viewers. There is a limit beyond which it can even appear menacing.

The gulf between the community of the living and the community of the dead cannot be bridged in the broad light of day. Nothing can help to close the gap save membership of the secret society.

*Discography*
*Musiques du Gabon*, OCR 41 (side B, séquence 2)

## The Zaire Basin

#### Kuyu (Fort-Rousset Region)

The ihuya masks were at one time used during the initiation cult devoted to the snake ancestor, Dyo. Since then, while they have become progressively deconsecrated, their original symbolism has not been entirely destroyed. Until a short time ago, the Kuyu society was divided into two clans, the Serpent people and the Panther people, between whom there existed both rivalries and alliances.

The Panther people had as an emblem a drum containing the skin of a big game animal. The sound box was decorated with variegated patterns representing the characteristic markings of the panther's skin.

The members of the Serpent clan made use of a series of sculptured statuettes. These were concealed under long skirts of woven raffia, and the wearers manipulated them in such a way as to evoke the movements of a snake.

The presentation of the ihuya to the apprentice initiates was carried out in successive stages corresponding to the different phases of creation.

239
240
241
Now that the traditional institutions of the clans have fallen into disuse, the old rivalries find their expression in a ritual contest, the Kyébé Kyébé. People from different villages are set opposite to each other in this dance. Each one of them must, in accordance with a rigid set of long-established traditional rules, perform a certain number of figures which are then judged on their suitability. The dancer holds by the sleeve a puppet that he moves up and down, backwards and forwards, all the while turning himself round and round in a tight circle until he falls exhausted to the ground. His movements are very rapid, but at the same time they must be smooth so that they suggest both the supple gliding of the ancestor and the whirling of a tornado.

### Discography

Anthologie de la vie africaine (sequence 23), Ducretet-Thomson, 320 C 126

### Batéké-Andjinighi (Ewo Region)

226
to 229
The dance of the 'body-guards', the ébanigl, is all that remains of the military power of the Batéké chiefs, who in past centuries, led by their king Makoko, fought and conquered the kingdoms of Kongo and Loango.

In former times this dance was part of an obedience ritual, the nkani. The ébanigi wore feather head-dresses or raffia caps and their bodies were coated with white clay, or pembé. They leapt around all over the place, brandishing their weapons and striking aggressive attitudes. Sometimes they hurled insults at each other. This grotesque ritual fight was in appearance a parody of their master's authority, but in fact the essential meaning of it was to reinforce the power of the chief and confirm the role that the ébanigi played in controlling the social and religious life of the realm.

### Bibliography

R. Lehuard, Statuaire du Stanley-Poll, Collection arts d'Afrique noire, Paris, 1974

### Discography

Gabon: Musique des Mitsogho et des Batéké, OCR 84

## The Kasai Region

### Zaire

### Bapendé (Tshikapa Region)

242
Typical features of the giphogo mask of the Bapende are the half-closed eyes, the prominent nose and the jutting chin. The ceremonial uses made of it do not belie its appearance.

This is a 'healing mask' which takes part in the 'millet dance', a crucial moment in the fertility rites. Its healing elements also make it an indispensable instrument in the annual purification ceremony of the village.

Giphogo is considered to be more than usually powerful and its benevolent influence extends over the cultivated fields and over all places inhabited by man. Its power is a reflection of that of the chief. The giphogo, leader of the masks, or Mukishi Wa Mutwe, when it is not 'coming out' is stored in the house of the one of whom it is the symbolic double. It is at the inauguration of this sanctuary, as well as at other times, that the mindgangi 243 masks of plaited fibre make their appearance. These beings are incarnations of the spirits of the ancestors and they are also the guardians of the circumcision enclosure. As initiators of the boys they teach them, by their presence, the respect due to all chiefs, both living and dead.

### Bakuba (Meshenge Region)

244
245
246
The mask mwaash a mbooy, or more correctly, mosh'ambooy mu shal, whose 'royal' dance marks the end of the initiation rites of the young boys, is associated with the creation myth and with the legend of the Kuba royalty. Woot, the great ancestor who taught all the skills of weaving and forging, completed the divine creation, and it is Woot who founded the dynasty.

The Nyim, kings of the Bakuba, were then recruited into the Bushoong clan and became the custodians of this fragment of divine power on earth.

Woot, the mythical hero, committed the original incestuous act, either with his daughter or with his sister, according to the different versions of the myth. One of these versions records the event in the following manner: 'One day when Woot was drunk with palm wine and lay naked on the ground, his sons started mocking him. Mweel, his daughter, came to him, walking modestly backwards, and covered him with a cloth made of raffia fibre. When Woot awoke, he rewarded her by declaring that he would have no other heirs but children of hers. As for his sons, their punishment was to submit to the rites of initiation.'

The ambooy mask is a representation of Woot and his divine successors. Another mask, the ngaadi mwaash, represents Mweel and the female members of the royal lineage.

The function of the male initiation and therefore of these two masks is to reinforce the authority of the king, who is descended from Woot, and to instil respect for the law that states that all property and power is transmitted through women.

The fragments of raffia stalks used for ambooy's face are a reminder of the intoxicating wine and the covering leaves of the original palm tree in the myth. And the cone shape that over-hangs the mask stands for the elephant's trunk, a symbol of power. The beads and cowries represent the king's wealth, and the eagle-feathered crest is the emblem of the royal Bushoong clan.

*Bibliography*

J. Vansina, 'Le royaume Kuba', Annales du MRAC, Tervuren, 1964

L. de Heusch, *Le roi ivre ou l'origine de l'état,* Gallimard, Paris, 1972

*Salampasu* (Luiza Region)

The high, rounded forehead and the overall shield shape appear to be constant stylistic features of the Salampasu masks, but 234 they can be classified into various categories in accordance with to 238 the material used to cover the masks and the accompanying accessories. Some are made of black plaited fibre and topped by a cone-shaped head-dress adorned with different coloured triangles. Others are wooden masks with wide tufts of feathers, and then there are the masks covered with strips of copper and crowned with pompoms made of plant fibre.

These masks take part in the male initiation rites. They are shown to the neophytes in a progressive order symbolizing the three ranks of society: the hunters, the warriors and the chief.

# Rwanda and the Uélé region

## Rwanda

*Tutsi* (Nyanza Region)

Before it attained independence in 1962, the kingdom of Rwanda included three ethnic groups differing in race, social status and economic role.

At the bottom of the social scale were the oldest inhabitants of the territory, the Twa, of pygmoid stock. They were for the most part hunters and they provided the farmers and the herdsmen with meat. To the latter they also paid tributes of skins and ivory.

Then came the farmers of Bantu stock, the Huttu. These formed eighty-two per cent of the population. And lastly, of a higher caste, were the Tutsi shepherds. These were of Ethiopian stock and were tall with delicate features.

The Tutsi, coming from the east, invaded the territory in the sixteenth century. They imposed a system of political and economic authority based on the ownership of cattle and on the exploitation of the other two groups.

At the top of this hierarchy of aristocratic families was the chief of the sacred royalty, the Mwami.

The royal drums, the ngoma, were symbols of his mystical 255 power, and the drum beaters belonged of necessity to the aristocracy. The Ntoré were also recruited from this caste. These 253 warriors protected the realm from cattle thiefs, and when they 254 returned from their missions they danced at the king's court, miming the courage and the spirit that they had shown in their fights.

*Discography*

*Musique du Rwanda,* BM 30 L 2302

## Zaire

*Mangbetu* (Nanga Region)

European travellers who visited the Mangbetu territory during the second half of the nineteenth century were astounded by the wealth of artistic expression in this region.

Architecture, furniture, weapons, agricultural implements, musical instruments, costumes and the body itself, all reveal a strong feeling for aesthetic values.

The chiefs of the Mangbetu clan, driven by the urge to exhibit their power and their aristocratic privileges, accorded an important role to the artists and craftsmen and thus promoted the development of applied arts.

In spite of the dismantling of the old political structure, certain aspects of this former splendour have survived until recently. The 'war dances', frequently described by nineteenth-century observers, extolled the memory of Mangbetu military prowess. The basketwork shields, so finely and strongly plaited, have disappeared, and more simply decorated wooden boards have taken their place. The fine ivory ceremonial horns have also 250 become rarer. But the energy displayed in the miming of the 252 fights still retains the old vigour. The aesthetic tradition of cranial modification continued up till the 'fifties. The process is begun in infancy by means of small raffia cords, and in addition to causing, through continuous pressure, an elongation of the skull, it results in the stretching of the eyelids and the raising of the eyebrows.

The oblong appearance of the head and face is still further emphasized among the women by a hairstyle in the form of a flared cylinder.

The negwé is an oval buttock cover made from sycamore bark 250

194

that has been beaten and dyed with earth, and the combination of colours and of geometrical patterns that adorn it is evidence of a vivid aesthetic imagination. The same complex patterns were to be found in the body paintings of the women, with their numerous abstract interlacing motifs.

*Mbuti* (Ituri Region)

The 'hunters and gatherers' who live in the heart of the dense Ituri forest do not regard their surroundings as an enemy. On the contrary, both their everyday behaviour and their ceremonial performances reveal their attitude of friendly respect towards the forest.

The environment is, in fact, not so hostile and inhospitable to the pygmy population as is commonly believed. The forest is the mother who nourishes and protects the people. Admittedly, these small groups of forest nomads can only eke out a precarious living, but this has not prevented them from developing a particularly rich and complex culture. The prodigious vocal polyphonies of the Pygmies have astonished Western musicologists, who have detected in their skilful contrapuntal harmonizing the equivalent of the many-voiced fugues of the classical era in Western music.

The reason for this flourishing of dance, music and song is to be found in the Mbuti concept of the world and of life.

230 The great ritual of atonement is the molimo madé. During this, to 233 fire, restorer of the hunters' prey, is lit and fed by young men who will judge and beat with cudgels those adults who have been guilty of offences against the forest divinity. It is this fire that endows the music and dance with its function of purification. The words spoken by the old Mbuti clearly establish the relationship between the composing of songs and the gratitude owed to the forest deity. 'All is well in our world but sometimes during the night unforeseen trouble may creep upon us. At dawn we arouse the forest with our songs as we wish the awakening to be joyful. Thus all will be well again.'

---

*Discography*
*La musique des Pygmées Babenzélé*, BM 30 L 2303

---

*Bakumu* (Madula Region)

The Bakumu, who live on the banks of the Tshopo a few kilometres south-east of Kisangani, seem to accord a great deal of significance to prophecy in their social and religious activities.

Thus the outings of the masks, the ritual dances that accompany the rites, the initiations and the funerals of members of the sect, are all placed under the authority of an association of 247 soothsayers: the Bafumu.
249 The masks, the nsembu, are seen mostly in couples of male 248 and female. Newly-initiated members of the sect join together in the kunda dance.

# Ubangui region

## Central African Empire

*Gbaya-Banda-Ngbaka* (Carnot, Bambio and Mbaïka Regions)

Each of the three tribes of Gbaya, Banda and Ngbaka has a distinct ethnic unity, but their initiation rites have numerous features in common. The name that is given to the three cultures is almost identical: gaza or ganza, 'that which gives force'.

The sequence of the initiation teaching and the ordeals of the gaza are practically the same in the three groups.

The first stage of initiation comprises tests of physical endurance and then admission, by means of songs, to the first degree of esoteric knowledge. The initiate learns the body techniques, in particular the different choreographic figures, and is also taught social behaviour.

The circumcision and excision rites mark the end of this period, which is spent outside the village and may last as long as several months.

The excised girls, the gazawoko or ganza Yassi, live in groups in huts on the outskirts of the village for a few weeks while waiting for the healing of their wounds. When the village is deserted because the men are working in the forest and the women are working in the manioc and groundnut fields, the 214 young girls make their way to the pools where they will take 213 their ritual bath. They will avoid all the paths where they might meet somebody. Gradually they liberate themselves from the guardianship of their initiators and acquire strength and autonomy. They harvest their own food, even though they are not yet allowed to prepare it. At sunset the gazawolo gather together again in a secluded place to perfect the dance movements that they will have to perform at the ceremonies ending their initiation.

These ceremonies will bring them into the full life of the community. During the course of the celebrations they will sing songs, to the accompaniment of the split drum, the linga, and 209 other percussion instruments, which evoke the memory of their 207 harsh life during the period of seclusion. The energy displayed in 208 the various dances will prove to everybody that the ordeals have been overcome and that the gaza has 'given them strength'. 202 to 207 210 to 212

---

*Discography*
*Musiques d'initiation*, (RCA) HM 934
*Musiques Banda*, (RCA) Vogue LD 765

---

204

217

219

218

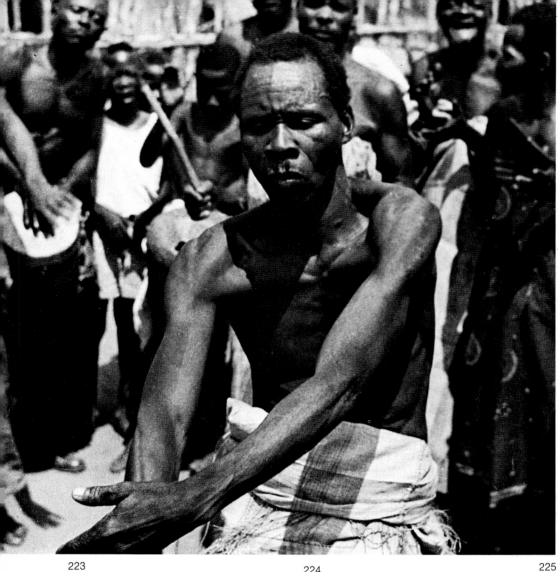

223

224

225

226

227

228

229

234

235

239

240    24

244

245

246

247

248

## Captions

**General Bibliography**  (The bibliographical and discographical sources that refer directly to the groups of photographs in question are included at the end of the relevant ethnographic notes.)

Robert Farris Thompson: *African Art in Motion*, VCLA, Los Angeles, 1974

Francis Bebey: *Musique de l'Afrique*, Horizons de France, Paris, 1969

Gilbert Rouget: 'La musique d'Afrique noire', in *Histoire de la musique*, vol.1, Encyclopédie de la Pleiade, NRF, Paris, 1960

Georges Balandier, Jacques Maquet and other collaborators: *Dictionnaire des civilisations africaines*, Fernand Hazan, Paris, 1968

Denise Paulme and Jacques Brosse: *Parures africaines*, Hachette, Paris, 1956

Roy Sieber: *African textiles and decorative arts*, Moma, New York, 1972

Herbert Cole: *African arts of transformation*, University of California, Santa Barbara, 1971

Jean Laude: *Les Arts de l'Afrique noire*, Le Livre de Poche, LGF, Paris, 1966

*The Arts of Black Africa*, University of California Press, Berkeley, 1971

Jacqueline Delange: *Arts et Peuples de l'Afrique noire*, NRF Gallimard, Paris, 1967

*The Arts and Peoples of Black Africa*, Dutton and Co., New York, 9174

Frank Willet: *African Art*, Thames and Hudson, London, 1971

Printed by Imprimerie Attinger
Neuchâtel, Switzerland
30 June 1978.